Magical Christianity

MAGICAL CHRISTIANITY

The Power of Symbols for Spiritual Renewal

COLESTON BROWN

QUEST

BOOKS

Theosophical Publishing House
Wheaton, Illinois • Chennai, India

First Quest Edition 2007

Quest Books
The Theosophical Publishing House
P. O. Box 270
Wheaton, IL 60189-0270

Cover image: *How at the Castle of Corbin a Maiden Bare in the Sangreal and Foretold the Achievements of Galahad,* by Arthur Rackham

www.questbooks.net

Cover design, book design, and typesetting by Dan Doolin

Library of Congress Cataloging-in-Publication Data

Whitehead, Nicholas.
Magical Christianity: the power of symbols for spiritual renewal / Coleston Brown. — 1st Quest ed.
    p.   cm.
Rev. ed. of: Patterns in magical Christianity / Nicholas Whitehead. c2002.
Includes bibliographical references and index.
ISBN-13: 978-0-8356-0855-8
ISBN-10: 0-8356-0855-7
1. Occultism—Miscellanea 2. Magic. 3. Magic—Religious aspects—Christianity. 4. Occultism—Religious aspects—Christianity. 5. Archetype (Psychology)—Miscellanea. 6. Symbolism (Psychology)—Miscellanea. I. Whitehead, Nicholas. Patterns in magical Christianity. II. Title.
BF1999.W536 2007
133.4'3—dc22   2006036107

5   4   3   2   1   *   07   08   09   10   11

Printed in the United States of America

Para Marina,
quien es
verdaderamente
un espíritu de luz

CONTENTS

Preface   ix

Author's Note   xi

Introduction   1

Chapter 1: The Sphere   13

Chapter 2: The Axis   25

Chapter 3: The Holy Fire   37

Chapter 4: The Center   55

Chapter 5: The Wheel of Life   71

Chapter 6: The Three Realms   97

Chapter 7: The Planes of Being   113

Chapter 8: The Miryam Tradition   129

Appendix: Kenosis   145

Notes   147

Selected Bibliography   165

Index   169

PREFACE

The impetus for this book goes back to 1978 when I embarked upon a course, run by Gareth Knight, in Christian Qabalistic magic. The course required building a series of symbolic images in the imagination. Several of these impressed me deeply at the time, for they seemed to carry some extraordinary power of regeneration.

Some years later, I rediscovered through conventional academic channels the notion that there are primordial "ideas" or archetypes common to, and at the root of, many spiritual and esoteric philosophies and practices worldwide. I was particularly intrigued by the fact that some of these archetypes manifested through symbols and patterns strikingly similar to the ones I had encountered in those early days of training.

This observation in turn sparked my subsequent research into the subject of this book—the role of certain archetypal patterns in Magical Christianity. A large portion of this research involved actual practical experience, by myself and others, employing specialized methods of ritual and inner vision.

I have attempted to combine the insights gained from this practical work with sound esoteric analyses of appropriate background material—traditions, texts, legends, myths, and symbols. The resulting text constitutes a practical introduction to Magical Christianity that I hope others will find as beneficial to read and work with as I did to prepare. Anyone interested in further details regarding Magical Christianity, or the Magical Way in general, is encouraged to visit my Web site, www.magicalways.com.

Coleston Brown
Feast of the Magi
Angel Fire, New Mexico
2007

Author's Note

This book presents a set of meditation exercises that are configured to enable the aspirant to experience the three primary methods of magic as taught in the mystery schools: meditation, pathworking or inner pilgrimage, and ceremonial ritual. Although these exercises have been carefully graded and tested, it must be added that they will not yield of their fruits unless rooted in the spirit of contemplation, that is, unless undertaken in a sense of loving service to Divine Being.

Students should practice each exercise for approximately two to three weeks, preferably twice a day. The exercises end with suggested ritual phrases that encapsulate the energies experienced in that exercise. Choose one for each exercise, and with a little practice you should soon be able to contact the relevant inner powers simply by reciting your phrase. The sequence of phrases as a whole thus becomes a kind of magical rosary or litany. Indeed, the suggested phrases appearing at the end of the exercises for the first six chapters are incorporated into the litany that forms the concluding practical work for the book.

Professional recordings giving expanded versions of most of the exercises with appropriate sound effects and music are included on the compact disc accompanying this book.

ℐNTRODUCTION

℃hristianity is a magical tradition. This is not so controversial a statement as some might think, for all spiritual traditions are potentially magical by the simple fact that they contain myths, legends, lore, and symbols that enable the mediation of spiritual energies between levels of reality.

The term "magical," then, refers to a power inherent in the structure of spiritual tradition—the power of *mediation*. And mediation by its very nature always involves or brings about some form of *transformation*. When we speak, therefore, of Magical Christianity, we mean approaching and employing the magical lore and symbolism preserved in the Christian tradition as a way of self-transformation and spiritual service. On one level this refers to a mystical transfiguration of the soul. On another it refers to an active and willing cooperation with the inner orders of beings under the Living Son of Light[1] in the transformation, redemption, or "christification" of the cosmos.

All this is implicit in the symbolic content or magical lore of the tradition itself. It will be useful, therefore, to begin our study by looking at the structure and import of magical symbols.

There are basically two types of magical symbols. There are *inner* or *imaginal symbols*, which are symbols built up or received through the inner senses, and *outer* or *material symbols*, which are symbols

1

(occurring either by design or in nature) that are experienced with the outer senses.[2]

It is possible for either an imaginal or a material symbol to become a vehicle for the direct expression of spiritual energy. It is usual, however, for the two types to appear in tandem. A material symbol will often have an imaginal counterpart and vice versa. Because of the more fluid structure of imaginal symbols, however, these tend to take a superior role, acting as bridges or transformers between the physical symbols and archetypal energy.

When this is the case, a practical situation arises that is analogous to a kind of three-stage funnel (figure 1). This funnel could be visualized with the upper, widest part originating in the realm of archetypal essence, the lower and narrower section marking the condensation of archetypal power in an imaginal form, and the tip of the funnel being the symbol or point of manifestation on the terrestrial plane.

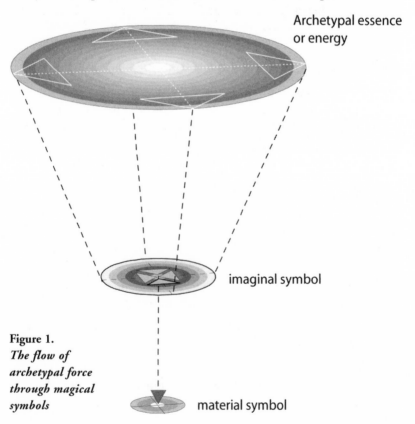

Archetypal essence or energy

imaginal symbol

Figure 1.
The flow of archetypal force through magical symbols

material symbol

Another useful analogy could be made with the stained glass windows of a church or cathedral. The pure light of the sun (archetypal essence or energy) passes through a translucent image (imaginal symbol), which transforms the light in such a way that it affects the physical environment and the consciousness of those who are in that environment (physical symbol).

This analogy is quite precise and is capable of considerable development. The position of the sun during the day and year, for instance, alters the luminosity of the window and hence the direction of light and emphasis of certain colors within the building.

Other factors worthy of meditation would be the play of light and darkness within the cathedral, or the fact that the light goes in from without during the day, yet out from within (assuming candles or other lights are present) during the night. Bearing in mind the two basic types of symbol and the roles they play in embodying archetypal energies, we make the following six statements about magical symbols in general:

1. Magical symbols are inherently appropriate.
2. Magical symbols always participate in a greater reality.
3. Magical symbols enable the translation of energies between levels of reality.
4. Magical symbols are transrational.
5. Magical symbols are polyvalent.
6. Magical symbols tend to assemble in groups expressing fields of energy.

Let us remark on these observations one by one.

1. *Magical symbols are inherently appropriate.* This statement simply means that a magical symbol is neither arbitrarily derived, nor the result of mere convention, for its innate form adequately expresses its meanings. Consider the image of a plant. Its roots are in the earth, its flower in the air; within its stem the life-bearing sap rises and falls. Because of its intrinsic structure, the plant is a symbol for the ideal spiritual life or growth of the human being. We live upon the earth, with our roots in the land. We are nurtured by the soil on which we live. Yet, without losing our connection with the soil, our destiny is to rise above the land, to flower in the crowning glory of the light. This flowering comes about as a combination of our own directed efforts—analogous to the growth of the stem and to the flow of water and sap within it—and the activity of the light of divine grace. For it is in response to that light that the flower of the spirit develops and unfolds.[3]

Again note that we cannot *make* the plant into a symbol. It simply *is* a magical symbol by virtue of its inherent structure and its role in the rhythmic life of the cosmos.

2. *Magical symbols participate in a greater reality.* Magical symbols always participate in a reality greater than themselves. This property of symbols enables us to gain access to other levels of reality. Such access might entail, for instance, an expansion of awareness on a "horizontal" plane—an experience of the inner aspects of nature, of other worlds or dimensions and the energies to be found there. A similar expansion might also occur on a "vertical" plane, with symbols acting as transformers for higher spiritual, or archetypal, essences.

Taking again the image of a plant, it is not difficult to see how it participates in something greater than itself, that is, the cosmic cycles of the day and the seasons. As a magical symbol, the plant embodies the movement and rhythms of the life force within the universe. It therefore acts as a bridge to analogous cycles and energies within human life and consciousness. The yearly cycle of vegetation resonates with the life cycle of the human being, not only physically, but psychically and spiritually. It is in fact a well-known magical practice to align oneself to the rhythms of the sun, the moon, the seasons, and stars. In so doing, one attempts to align oneself to the circuit of life force within the cosmos, to become at one with nature in all its visible and invisible aspects.

On the other hand, the growth direction of a plant is vertical. This vertical or axial "destiny" is directly analogous to the spiritual destiny of humankind. Just as a plant is destined to rise between earth and sky, dependent upon the influence of both for its existence, so does human consciousness stand between the elemental world and the realm of pure spirit. Ultimately, having aligned ourselves with divine will, it is our spiritual destiny to become participants in the restoration of a broken world, even to become coredemptors of all creation.

3. *Magical symbols enable the translation of energies between levels of reality.* Another thing we can say about magical symbols is that they always involve the translation of energies between one level of reality and another. Magical symbols are by nature the agencies of mediation. Among other things, magical technique involves interacting with symbols by using the inner senses: the inner vision, the inner sense of touch, taste, hearing, smell. These inner senses have a natural connection with the outer, physical senses (in fact, they are the same senses "inturned") and hence with the physical body as a whole, the instrument of our outer experience.

What this means is that whenever the inner senses are used by a trained adept—every time one participates in a magical symbol on inner levels, every time one contacts energy inwardly—there inevitably occurs a translation of this energy to the outer world.

It is a misunderstanding and misuse of this principle of mediation that has given rise to the spate of books and courses that teach one how to obtain personal and financial success through techniques of visualization, "positive thinking," and so on. And it is a dim intuition of this same process that has yielded the endless platitudes and semitechniques that revolve around the New Age maxim "you create your own reality."

Rightly understood and applied, however, the principle of mediation transforms one's daily experience, sanctifies it with meaning. A great portion of one's life becomes a kind of spiritual exercise. This does not mean that one's experiences are necessarily any different outwardly than anybody else's. It is that they tend towards a holism, a totality, full-lived in spiritual significance.

4. *Magical symbols are transrational.* Our fourth observation about the nature and function of magical symbols is that they are transrational. On one level this simply means the significance of magical symbols cannot be grasped by purely intellectual means. They must be experienced, actually participated in, if they are to be understood.

A simple analogy could be found in imagining that you have been given the task of helping a blind person who has suddenly gained sight to cope with and understand the experience of seeing color.

Could you do this by reciting the scientific theories of optics or the refraction of light, or by describing the principle of a spectrum to this person? Would it not be far more effective if you were to proceed, for instance, by describing green as the color of grass, by having this person touch grass first, then identify its color as green? In other words, the path of the intellectual processes can yield very different results from that of actual experience.

Knowing the theories or explanations of color or of magical symbols is a far cry from experiencing of color or symbols.

The transrational property of symbols extends beyond consideration of the limitations of the intellectual function. It is important to realize that we are talking about a mode of apprehension and understanding that takes place on an entirely different level of awareness. Symbols often present paradoxical experiences or experiences of reality that are capable of being apprehended only *through symbols*. Two examples will suffice.

One of the esoteric traditions states that the way to the stars is through the center of the earth. Now, this statement is not logical, at least not in any merely intellectual or rational sense. Yet magical tradition holds that it is no meaningless conundrum but rather a paradox of profound significance—a significance that can only be grasped through symbols. True, on one level it does serve to convey an important magical principle, namely, that the deepest levels of reality are also the highest. But unless this principle is something we have actually experienced, the explanation merely replaces one paradox with another. The only way to fully grasp the meaning of this tradition is to approach it from an entirely different level than that of the discursive, rational mind.

Let me describe the kind of inner scenario that might enable this kind of experience. You could, for example, visualize yourself in a cavern deep within the heart of the earth. Looking down you see that there is a small hole in the floor. Through this hole you see innumerable stars spread throughout the reaches of space. By meditating on this vision, by feeling yourself in the cave, looking at the stars, it is possible to experience certain inner aspects of reality that cannot be grasped through the reasoning processes. These inner aspects may relate to the relationship between crystals and stars, to various levels of being or of the cosmos, or to something else entirely. The structure of this exercise itself provides the means by which a person may grasp, more or less directly, the reality behind the paradox.

The second example is an anecdote or legend about Alanus ab Insula, also known as Alain de Lille. Alanus is regarded as one of the really great poets of the Middle Ages, and he was known as *doctor universalis*, a master teacher who was conversant in all the known fields of learning of his time.

Alanus lived and taught in Paris in the latter part of the twelfth century. One evening he was walking along the Seine River mulling over the subject of his lecture to be given the next morning. He was to talk on the nature of Divine Being. As he walked along thinking of an appropriate approach to his subject, he noticed a young boy playing in the sand near the edge of the river.

The little boy had dug a small hole in the sand, and he was happily filling it with water, which he carried over from the river in a wooden spoon. Alanus stopped and, having mentioned who he was and what he was about, stood watching the boy's play for a while.

Intrigued by the strange activity, Alanus finally asked him what he was doing. The boy replied that he was going to pour all the water of the river into the hole he had dug. With a patronizing smile, Alanus remarked that this would be quite impossible. One could not possibly pour all the water of the river into that little hole! The boy seemed thoughtful for a moment, then looking the great doctor full in the face, replied that it would be equally impossible for Alanus to speak about the nature of God!

Alanus was totally shattered. Reeling from the immensity of the truth spoken by the child, he staggered off home without a further word. The next day he showed up at the lecture hall as expected. But instead of beginning his lesson, he turned to the students, tore his outer robe from his body, and walked out, never to return. It is said that he eventually entered a monastery and there carried out the duties of a shepherd.

We can see how this story illustrates that symbols operate beyond the level of mere discursive reasoning. The image of the child trying to pour the Seine into a little hole conveys far more about the mystery of God, of Universal Being, about the relationship between Ultimate Being and human consciousness, than volumes of learned intellectual postulations possibly could. We see how a symbol can convey in a split second so profound a revelation that it radically transforms one's outlook.

5. *Magical symbols are polyvalent.* Our fifth statement about magical symbols is that they are polyvalent. The term comes from *poly*, "many," and *valens*, which translates as "value," "worth," or "meaning." In other words, a symbol cannot be fully understood by any single meaning, or on any one level of experience. A symbol always participates in a spectrum of significance, an entire range of meaning.

The characteristic symbols have of revealing several meanings at once suggests that symbols participate in more than one "system" or archetypal pattern at the same time. Take, for instance, the image of fire. As a symbol of the power of God, fire manifests both divine justice and divine illumination (it can blast as well as bless) — two essentially opposite meanings. But fire will also be found expressing many nuances of meaning between these two extremes: as a symbol of the divine presence (as in the burning bush, for instance), or of the warm, nurturing womb; the Blessed Heart or Cosmic Center (as in the hearth fire); or again as a symbol of wisdom, knowledge, passion, or purification. Magical symbols are thus like multifaceted jewels or many-branched trees.

In practical terms this quality enables us to experience a wide range of related inner energies simultaneously. To some degree also, the polyvalence of symbols accounts for the apparent differences in reaction among a group of people to any given magical or mystical working. There is a kind of protective or selective power operative in the structure of magical symbols by which, for any of a large number of reasons, various levels of conscious inner experience may be closed to one person yet open to another.

6. *Magical symbols tend to assemble in groups expressing fields of energy.* In actual experience magical symbols rarely appear as single, isolated images. They are often grouped together in significant ways. Most magical workings make use of a certain range of symbolism, a certain group of meaningfully interrelated images and actions. We call such groups "symbolic fields" because the symbols used in any magical operation constitute a unique array of inner energies—a field—that has a specific effect on consciousness and matter. By this we do not mean to imply that there are rigid rules or recipes that can be applied mechanically to yield a desired effect. The practical development of a symbolic field (as in a magical journey or ritual) is rather like the creation of a painting, poem, or other work of art: It is the product of a balanced mix of technical expertise, intuitive perception, and inspired activity.

Symbolic fields are of two main types. First is the *magical glyph*, which consists of a particular dominant or central image together with a set of subsymbols that cohere through their shared resonance or "vibration" with the dominant image. Examples of magical glyphs might be found in any of the Tarot images, for instance, where a central figure is given certain accoutrements, is associated with a symbolic landscape, stands in a certain pose, and so on. Other examples are to be found in the icons and statuary of shrines and temples, in the structure of myth and legend, and in certain forms of inner journey.

The second class of symbolic field is the *magical pattern*. Magical patterns are of a nature more complex than magical glyphs and indeed are often composed of a set of glyphs arranged according to some archetypal pattern of relationships (usually in the form of numerical or geometric configurations).

They might well, in fact, be termed "master glyphs." Examples are the Qabalistic Tree; the sequence of the Tarot trumps; sacred features in the landscape; certain temples, churches, and cathedrals; the magic wheel or circle; and the zodiac. Indeed, the inherent character of this latter symbolic field, the great round of the zodiac, provides a useful analogy for understanding the relationship among magical patterns, magical glyphs, and magical symbols: The individual stars are like magical symbols, the constellations are glyphs, and the zodiac as a whole is a magical pattern.

Meditation upon this analogy will be repaid with insight.

* * * * * * *

All theoretical knowledge regarding the structure and function of magical symbols is pointless unless given practical expression. In the Western mysteries such practical work is based upon the techniques of magic.

Many people are shocked by the use of Christian material for magical purposes. But this reaction is merely the result of a fearful misunderstanding of the Magical Way. Magic is a means of bringing about transformation (some would say transformation in consciousness) through the mediation of spiritual energies. A mage is above all a mediator. And in the Western tradition of the mysteries of the Son of Light, a mage is a mediator who in companionship with others—masters, saints, angels, mages, etc.—works to bring about the restoration or redemption of the world in both its inner and outer aspects. In this sense, magic is a specialized form of service to God and one's fellow creatures.

The Magical Way is universal in scope. Its practitioners, in accordance with the belief that Christ came not to condemn the old way but to fulfill it, work in many spiritual traditions and within many cycles of legend and mythology. These traditions function as doorways to the inner side of creation, portals to unseen energies and entities. Such matters are not undertaken with any sense of missionary zeal. Nor are there unbalanced attempts at "converting" others (whether they be resident on the outer or the inner planes). The true mage works in an attitude of selfless compassion, bringing healing and balance to little-recognized areas of creation. Indeed, many who work with the material in this book are not Christians, in the sense of being adherents of particular religious doctrines or belief structures. (Some, of course, are, and some even are clerics in religious organizations.)

Because of this inherent nonsectarian and universal spirit, what we have called Magical Christianity is really but one area of experience within the primordial tradition of the mysteries of the Son of Light. It is, however, the most important area of experience for most Westerners, providing a clear link to the universal mystery tradition through specific images and patterns that are deeply embedded in what the Renaissance mages termed the *anima mundi*, which might be roughly described as the "group soul" of the West.

Magical Christianity is not a new religion; it is not even a new aspect of an old religion. It is a specialized aspect of the universal tradition, which has been present within Christianity from the start. It may not have been always clearly visible, or readily identifiable or accessible, but it has always been present. And so it will continue, *mutatis mutandis*, as long as there are dedicated souls willing and able to take up the spark of inspiration, fan it into flame, and pass on the torch to others.

The purpose of this book is to present certain aspects of Christian magical lore. It has also been our intent to set forth a series of practical exercises that will provide a cornerstone of inner experience for those who seek initiation into the deep and fulfilling way of self-transformation and spiritual service that is the Magical Way of the mysteries of the Son of Light.

The **S**PHERE

"In the beginning God created the heaven and the earth. And the earth was without form, and void; and darkness was upon the face of the deep. And the Spirit of God moved upon the face of the waters" (Gen. 1:1–3).

In his commentary on this opening passage of Genesis, James of Edessa (ca. 535) remarks that the earth was originally formless because it was surrounded by the primordial sea "like the embryo is surrounded by the membranes in its mother's womb." He goes on, "Now God rent this primordial sea. Then he ordered the earth to give up its character of a smooth globe; and he made protuberances and holes, heights and depths on its surface so that the waters were gathered and taken from its surface and the earth could appear."[1]

Two aspects of James's exegesis interest us in particular. One, he draws an analogy between the proto-earth and an embryo, thus evoking the image of a cosmic womb. And two, the earth was originally a perfect sphere. As we shall see, the images of cosmic womb and globe hold special initiatory importance, for they symbolize at one and the same time primordial wholeness, latent potentiality, and realized perfection.

An image closely related to the cosmic womb and sphere is the cosmic egg.[2] It is worth commenting that in Hebrew the word (*rahaf*) for the moving of the Spirit of God over the waters, means not only "moving" but also "brooding" or "hatching," suggesting that the Genesis myth was, indeed, at one time expressed through the image of a cosmogonic egg. Moreover, the passage in Genesis 1 in which God separates the upper and lower waters by creating the firmament easily evokes the image of a cosmic dome or sphere.

As far as Christianity is concerned, the myth of Genesis has always provided the general pattern for the cosmogonic sequence. However, this pattern was sharpened, defined, and focused through influences best characterized as Orphic. The impact of the Greek traditions of Orphic mysticism on the pictorial representations of Christ in the catacombs is well known. Less well known is the influence of Orphism on early Christian perceptions regarding the structure and symbolic "shape" of the cosmos.

According to Orphic myth, in the beginning was chaos, being neither light nor darkness, neither dry nor moist, neither hot nor cold; all was formless, unbounded, undifferentiated substance. Yet chaos itself was eventually contained or bound in the shape of a great egg. The egg divided and the primal, androgynous being—Phanes, the Shining One—was born.

At that moment the Three Cosmic Regions (or Realms) and the four elements came into being. The upper hemisphere of the cosmic egg became the dome of the heavens, while the lower hemisphere became the bowl of the UnderRealm and the foundation for the Terrestrial Region.

Disregarding for the moment the figure of Phanes, we observe that the imagery presented above is generally consonant with the Old Testament traditions which, as we have said, were the source *sine qua non* for early Christian conceptions about the genesis and structure of the cosmos. Not only do we have a common image of creation through separation, but the doctrine of Three Cosmic Regions was known to nearly all ancient cultures and forms part of the cosmological model that runs through both the Old and New Testaments.

During the long course of Christian tradition and visionary experience, we are not surprised to find the cosmic images of egg and sphere cropping up often, sometimes closely and consciously associated with each other.[3] The *Recognitions* and *Homilies* ascribed to Clement of Rome (ca. AD 99) both recount the Orphic cosmogony using the terms for "egg" and "globe" interchangeably.[4]

In the work *De imagine mundi* (ca. 1125), Honorius of Autun writes that the spherical universe resembles an egg, not only in shape, but in content. Different cosmic zones are reflected in the shell, albumen, and yoke of the egg, for instance,[5] In her earlier visions, as recorded in the *Scivias*,[6] Hildegard of Bingen (1100–1181) saw the cosmos in the shape of an egg, while in her later visions the image of a sphere occurs.

The sphere figures in the works of other great mystics and thinkers too. Julian of Norwich, in her *Showings* (ca. 1423), relates how during one of her visionary experiences she became aware of a small object "as round as any ball" resting in her hand. "What is it?" she asked. And the answer came: "It is everything which is made."[7]

The great *doctor universalis*, Alain de Lille (d. 1203), drawing on little-known hermetic traditions, wrote a treatise on the "intelligible sphere whose center is everywhere and whose circumference is nowhere."[8]

Taken purely in terms of its geometry, the sphere is the symbol of wholeness and primal totality par excellence. Its significance as a symbol of perfect balance derives from its "isotropic" nature. That is, it possesses the same properties in all directions. In a sense, the sphere contains within itself all other figures,[9] for, given equal surface area, a sphere has greater volume than any other shape.[10] At this level, the sphere signifies undifferentiated possibility.

The idea of latent potentiality is further suggested by the fact that a sphere has no determined axis. When a sphere is defined by an axis, then it can be said to represent the manifestation or actualization of possibility. Creation takes place, therefore, when the primordial sphere or cosmogonic egg is fixed along an axis.

The idea of such a Cosmic Axis takes many forms in the various traditions: a sacred pole or tree (e.g., the Cross, the Universal Tree); a sword, spear, pillar, tower, or mountain; or, as in the Orphic mysteries

and in esoteric Christian circles, a divine being. Sometimes, in myth
and symbol, the presence of the Axis is more subtly disclosed through
images such as the separation of the two halves of the cosmogonic egg,
or the elongation of the primordial sphere. Both these symbolic movements—separation and elongation—yield, it need hardly be said, an
ovoid configuration. This more typical egg-like shape relates, in a very
practical, esoteric sense, to the aforementioned pattern of three inter-
penetrating cosmic zones.[11]

It will be noted again that the image of the cosmic womb also
partakes of the sphere's sacred geometry (through the roundness of
pregnancy), just as, especially in relation to the mysteries of creation,
birth, and rebirth, it shares in the symbolism of the cosmic egg. Up to
a point, then, these three images—the sphere, the womb, the egg—
are interchangeable. During certain ceremonies, for instance, both the
Pueblo and the Pawnee Indians employ two bowls, one inverted over
the other, to represent the spherical cosmos.[12] For the Pueblo, at least,
this image is also linked to the concept of the cosmic womb (figure 2).

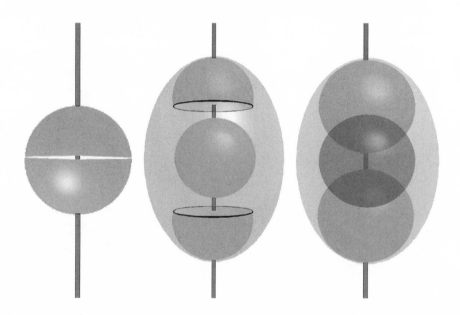

Figure 2. *The sphere, the egg, and the Three Cosmic Regions*

Among the Pueblo too, the connection extends to sacred architecture. The ceremonial lodges, known as *kivas*, are round, semi-subterranean structures obviously based upon the pattern of an earth womb.

A similar pattern is probably the basis for the thousands of prehistoric mound burials found by European settlers along the river valleys of eastern North America. The bodies were sometimes placed in a flexed, fetal position as if being returned to the cosmic womb that they might be ready for rebirth. In fact, the Choctaw Indians referred to the larger mounds as "navels."[13]

These patterns of sphericity and of birth and rebirth, no matter what mythic image or combination of images may have originally articulated them, lie at the root of similar burial structures known from earliest times in Europe, Asia, and the Middle East. We need only cite the numerous burial mounds of the Neolithic period in Europe, the *tholoi* or "beehive" tombs that are found all over the ancient Mediterranean world, the reliquary stupas distributed throughout the Buddhist world, the round tombs of North Africa, and the rock-cut domical tombs that occur widely in the Middle East and whose form was adopted and widely used throughout the Roman Empire. The widespread occurrence in the Hellenistic period of such structures provided a ready store of architectural symbolism for the early Christian masons and builders.

The earliest extant Christian burials, those in the catacombs, are associated with the egg and the sphere through the dome and arch forms that appear in connection with them, and also through the presence of eggshells in some of the graves. They are likewise connected to the symbolism of the cosmic womb through the caves themselves. The cavern has long been treated in sacred lore as the womb of the Earth Mother. It is of interest to note that there is beneath the Church of the Nativity at Bethlehem a sacred cave where, according to a well-known tradition of great antiquity, Christ was born of the Virgin Mother.

At any rate, the cosmic symbolism and function of these underground complexes was transferred above ground and merged with the existing Roman and Middle Eastern forms to yield the elaborated symbolic developments incorporated into the first churches. Most early Christian churches were either aisled basilicas or domed *martyria*. In the latter, a number of the martyrs' graves have been found to contain small marble eggs.

The *martyria* were certainly based upon the patterns infused into the architecture of the original Holy Sepulcher in Jerusalem. This church, like all sacred enclosures and edifices, replicated the structure of the cosmos. The upper dome, representing the starry heavens, and accordingly decorated with stars, sat upon a lower rotunda (representing the physical plane) marked with a niche at each of the cardinal directions. At the center of the rotunda was a shrine or edicule leading down to the actual cavern-tomb of Christ, representing the entrance to the UnderRealm.

The same symbolism resurfaces, transformed, in the churches of the Romanesque and Gothic periods, where it is expressed primarily through the vault, the arch (including the arched portals), the tower, the cruciform nave, the subterranean crypt, and, in a special way, in the Gothic rose windows. The ideal Gothic cathedral has three rose windows representing, among other things, the Three Cosmic Regions. At Chartres, for example, the focus of the northern window is the Christ Child, that is, the incarnated Logos in the Terrestrial Region. The western rose—the West is traditionally one of the points of entry to the UnderRealm—depicts Christ in judgment over the dead. The rose of the South, place of celestial fire and spirit, shows the ascended Christ in majesty over the cosmos.

The symbolism underlying the configuration of windows in a Gothic cathedral is complex and profound. We note here, however, that the eastern walls in Gothic cathedrals and churches do not generally sport rose windows. What does commonly appear is a single or connected series of relatively narrow, tall windows suggesting the symbolism of pillar or axis. Even when taken simply in terms of position and shape, these windows reflect two major themes closely linked to the mystery of cosmic redemption: the theme of the rebirth of creation, filtered through the symbolism of the East as the beginning point of the diurnal and seasonal cycles, and the theme of realignment of the Three Cosmic Regions through the axial power of the "resurrection body" of Christ. Indeed, eastern windows sometimes do depict the resurrected Christ.

According to ancient Christian tradition, the universe was created at Eastertide.[14] Christ's Resurrection, then, in that it brought about the birth of a "new creation," reiterates, on a higher octave, the primeval cosmogonic process.[15] Now, this idea of a new creation carries within it the possibility of the spiritual rebirth, that is, the initiation, of the individual soul. It is precisely because the domed, tombed churches embodied the archetypal structures of a redeemed or perfected cosmic order that they became the favored places for the initiation rites. The identification of the baptismal font itself with the bowl or *krater* of the UnderRealm or UnderEarth enabled the candidate to ritually enact the mysteries of Christ's descent to the UnderRealm and subsequent resurrection. This is clearly implied by the following article from the Council of Toledo (633): "The immersion in water is as a descent to the underworld, and the coming forth again from the water is a resurrection."[16]

To a large extent, the themes of creation and resurrection underlie the numerous rites and traditions which have accrued around Easter eggs. One or two examples from the vast treasure house of traditional lore will suffice to illustrate our point. At Easter Mass, during the Middle Ages, it was customary to have colored eggs near the altar. One of these would be placed in a model "tomb" and then removed by the priests at the appropriate moment. As this was done, the ritual phrase "Christ is risen" would be recited.[17] We might also note William of Normandy's thirteenth-century comparison of the emergence of a chick from an egg to the resurrected Christ bursting forth from the tomb,[18] and a rather striking image, occurring on a font at Alsleben bei Zerbst in Germany, shows Christ at the Resurrection emerging from an egg.[19]

One recalls in all of this the mythical Phanes from the Orphic tradition, who sprang from the Egg of Creation. It is important to note that Phanes, like Adam and numerous other primal ancestors, is androgynous, one in whom the male-female polarities are united, a "total" being. This notion of primordial wholeness underpins a great complex of spiritual traditions and techniques worldwide. In certain

Chinese myths, for example, the two sexes were originally embodied in the precosmic "breathing" which eventually formed itself into a great egg. From the egg, the cosmic regions of heaven and earth were then born. This myth has been linked to Taoist meditation techniques said to aid the initiate in achieving "immortality."[20]

The theme of the union of opposites in relation to the "resurrection body," which forms an important aspect of esoteric Christian teaching and practice, is too complex and extensive to be taken up in detail at this time. We will content ourselves, therefore, with a few key remarks. The coincidence of opposites is implicit, for example, in certain Eastern Orthodox icons representing Christ surrounded by a sphere of light, particularly at the Nativity, Transfiguration, Resurrection, and Ascension. We need hardly repeat here the significance of the sphere as a symbol of primordial totality, wholeness, perfection, and so on.

A similar iconography occurs in the Western church, though here the idea of the resolution of opposites is usually represented in the underlying geometry of the mandorla, the almond of light that surrounds the figure of the resurrected Christ. This shape is most simply generated by the intersection of two circles (figure 3), a figure also known as a *vesica piscis*.

Figure 3. *A vesica piscis*

The mandorla or *vesica piscis* thus signifies the integral nature of the Resurrected One who, because all opposites are united in him, embodies the characteristics of a "third race" in which "there is no male and female"[21] (Gal. 3:28): "All those will be astonished that see me. For from another race am I," say the Odes of Solomon (Ode 41) in reference to the initiatory experience in an early esoteric Christian community. The language is poetic and metaphoric, and at the same time symbolic and practical. We do well to keep in mind, however, that there is little correspondence here with the thin notions of popular psychology or New Age teachings regarding "getting in touch" with one's male or female side. The "language of androgyny" is an ancient esoteric convention and refers to the union, balancing, or resolution of all those forces within and without the human soul that tend, otherwise, to a state of polarization or conflict.

The idea of perfect wholeness contained within the symbolism of egg and sphere also finds expression in the clairvoyant perception of the human aura. The aura is generally described as an ovoid or spherical emanation of light encompassing the human form. According to esoteric teaching, the aura is at once the residue of man's primordial wholeness and the archetype of restored perfection. It is both a remnant of the "Adamic state" that existed before the human constitution divided into opposites[22] and the ultimate pattern of regeneration in Christ, who is "the new Adam." It is therefore not surprising that those with developed clairvoyant powers are able to sense or "see" in the aura the physical, psychic, and spiritual health of an individual.

Such perception normally takes the form of colors, shades, movements, and patterns of light in the aura. These observations are then interpreted by means of their inherent symbolism in ways that describe the various areas of balance and imbalance within the person. It is also possible to effect healing or changes in consciousness by visualizing changes in the hue, position, shape, or fluctuation of the auric light.

All valid esoteric work has a practical, experiential dimension. And, indeed, underpinning the theoretical content of this chapter (as of all the chapters) are certain principles that can only be fully realized from within the crucible of actual inner experience. Let us therefore practice the following exercise.

VISION EXERCISE ⌐ CD Track 2

The Sphere of Creation

*U*se the kenosis meditation (see appendix) to enter the deep peace. Become aware, deep within your being, of a tiny spark of light. This spark grows into a sphere that expands to encompass you and fill the cosmos.

Visualize the upper half of the cosmic sphere as gold, the lower half as silver. The sphere now turns indigo blue and you become aware of the shining stars all around you.

A landscape solidifies. You stand upon a plateau at the summit of a mountain. Near you runs a stream, soon becoming a river that empties into a great sea.

The full moon rises from your right and illumines the landscape with its silvery light. It sets to your left. At the point where the moon rose, the sun now rises, glorifying all the world with new light and life. You hear birds singing their dawn chorus. You become aware of a great host of angelic beings all around you and you commune with them. The sun sets and the sphere darkens again.

The sphere contracts, drawing the stars together so that their lights merge and you are at the center of a sphere of pure starlight that coincides with the boundary of your aura. You meditate upon this, repeating to yourself as you do so an appropriate ritual phrase (suggestions: "a shining sphere of cosmic love," "blessed are those who are centered in love," or "be hallowed by a sacred sphere").

The AXIS

Many early Christian churches had round apertures, openings to the sky, located at the center of their domes. One can imagine the interior of one of these churches lit by the beam of sunlight that entered through the *oculus* during the morning hours, and that at midday would shine straight down upon the central altar in a great column of light.

The column of light constitutes, so to speak, a Cosmic Axis. This *axis mundi* occurs in the guise of many other images in the Christian tradition, such as, the Paradisal Tree, the ladder, the mountain, the pillar, the stellar ray, the lance or spear, the staff and the crosier, the bell tower, the spire, and so on. All of these images, moreover, may be subsumed in the symbolism of the cross of Christ and, ultimately, to the very body of Christ. It will be well worthwhile to look more closely at some of these symbols as a prelude to our summary of the esoteric significance and spiritual function of the Cosmic Axis.

The Cosmic Tree is a primordial image, almost universally disseminated in both time and space. Its general symbolism reveals an image of the magical structure of the cosmos. The trunk, through which passes the rise and fall of the vital sap, stretches upward through the middle, earthly plane. The roots, drawing nutrients from the deep earth, represent the levels, stages, and grades of descent into the UnderRealm, just as the branches yielding leaf and fruit above show the stages of ascent through the heavens.

From time immemorial, the cosmic schema reflected in the Universal Tree has provided a means of orientation toward spiritual beings and sacred powers, as well as an itinerary for passage between one cosmic plane or region and another. When the Altaic shaman climbs his seven-notched birch pole, he simultaneously ascends, in vision, the Cosmic Tree through the celestial planes.[1] A similar symbolism comes into play among the Pueblo Indians of New Mexico whose sacred *kivas* are entered and exited by a ladder that extends through a central hole in the roof. Origen and Celsus mention the use in the Mithraic mysteries of a ladder of seven rungs of seven different metals. The rungs represent the different heavens through which the initiate ascends in order to attain the Empyrean.[2]

In the Old Testament we read of Jacob's dream of a ladder reaching from earth to heaven and "the angels of God were ascending and descending on it" (Gen. 28:10 ff).

In the Christian tradition, the ladder[3] has a long history. We must emphasize that wherever it occurs, almost without exception, from earliest times right through the Middle Ages, the image of the ladder retains its practical dimension as a means of mystical ascent and descent. Thus it is said that a sixth-century Irish bishop, Maedoc of Ferns, one day ascended a golden ladder reaching from earth to heaven. When he returned his face shone with a dazzling light.[4] In the twelfth century, Honorius of Autun describes the mode through which the soul attains visions of the different heavens and ultimately knowledge of God as a "great heavenly ladder" of ordered, congruent grades or rungs, a ladder that rises from earth to heaven and that if ascended in the correct manner leads to the vision of "the kingdom of glory in all its beauty."[5]

From early times too, Jacob's Ladder was associated with the Cross. "The Cross . . . is the ladder of Jacob with angels ascending and descending upon it, with the Lord standing at the uppermost rung," writes an anonymous Greek at the beginning of the third century.[6]

Drawing on the same body of traditions, Andrew of Crete (ca. 625), remarks that "the Cross is a ladder leading to heaven."[7] According to Theophanes Keramous (ca. 1135), when "Jacob lay down to sleep upon the stone, there was shown to him in a vision a ladder which extended from earth through all the spheres of the heavens. . . . To the eye of the soul, this ladder clearly figures the Cross."[8]

It is also worth noting that in some renditions the Cross is shown with seven notches along the upright suggesting, in a remarkable parallel to the notched pole of the shamans, a sevenfold hierarchy of celestial planes and powers.[9] This sevenfold pattern of ascensional symbolism has always played an important part in magical Christian practice. In modern times it is generally incorporated into the tenfold pattern of spheres and energies known as the Qabalistic Tree (figure 4).

Figure 4. *One version of the Qabalistic Tree*

Rightly understood, this very practical and inherently flexible glyph provides a means of orientation towards the beings and forces of the inner creation and a way of approaching the stages of mystical ascent.

Returning to the general symbolism of the Cosmic Tree, let us remark that the Tree not only presents an analog for the threefold structure of the cosmos but also embodies the vital processes of periodic renewal and regeneration that pervade the entire creation. This is one reason the Tree is almost universally associated with the idea of spiritual transformation. It is also why in the Christian tradition the Cosmic Tree is so closely tied to the symbolism of the Cross and hence to the redemption of Adam and the resurrection of Christ (figure 5).

Figure 5. *The Cross as the Tree of Life* (from a Spanish manuscript)[10]

According to one set of traditions, when Adam was near death he asked his son Seth to journey to Eden to obtain the fruit of immortality from the Paradisal Tree. He was able to acquire, however, only three seeds, which were given to him by the archangelic guardian of paradise. These he placed under Adam's tongue. Though Adam died three days later, the seeds sprouted from his grave, yielding three trees growing so close together that they merged into one.[11] Adam's body was taken aboard the ark by Noah and was eventually buried at Golgotha. After many adventures, including its incorporation into the lintel of the Temple of Solomon,[12] and its use as a rod of healing by David, the wood of the Paradisal Tree was used to make the Cross of the Crucifixion. And as Christ's side was pierced with the Lance of Longinus, his blood spilled upon Adam's skull and Adam was thus redeemed.[13]

A considerable amount of esoteric wisdom may be gleaned from this cycle of legends. What concerns us for the moment, however, is the clear link established between the Cosmic Tree and the cross of Christ. For it is only with an awareness of these two as expressions of the Cosmic Axis that certain elements of the redemptive, healing, and regenerative powers traditionally assigned to the symbol and sign of the Cross in Magical Christianity can be fully understood.

Another line of tradition links the Universal Axis to the Incarnation by tracing the history of a staff made from the wood of the Paradisal Tree. This staff, bearing the secret name of God upon it, was brought out of the Garden of Eden by Adam, from whom it descended to Enoch, Noah, Shem, Abraham, Jacob, and Joseph, eventually reaching Jethro, the priest of Median. One day, Jethro stuck the staff into the earth and was unable to draw it out again, and "all the strong men in Median came and tried to pull it out, yet none succeeded." It was only Moses who was able to draw forth the staff from the ground, and with it he performed many miracles and feats of magic. The staff was handed down until it reached David. After David it continued to be passed on, but the recipients or heirs were now no longer aware of the power and history of the staff.[14] At last it reached the hands of Joseph the Carpenter, for whom it suddenly blossomed forth as a sign for all that he was the one chosen to wed the Virgin Mary. The symbol of the blossoming staff touches upon a doctrine of considerable importance in esoteric Christian tradition, namely, that Christ himself "incarnates" the Cosmic Axis.[15]

We note again the appearance of Jacob among those who inherited the holy staff. We have already seen the importance that Jacob's Ladder has as an expression of the Cosmic Axis. Indeed, this correspondence is emphasized even more when we consider the tradition that after his dream, Jacob set up the stone on which he had laid his head as a pillar shrine to God (Gen. 28:18). Obviously, a complex iconography surrounds the figure of Jacob and his relation to the Axis. He was, for instance, the father of the twelve tribes of Israel, which on one level makes him the center of a zodiacal arrangement of territory and lineage. Moreover, the episode where he bows his head over his staff to bestow his blessings upon the sons of Joseph (Gen. 47:31, Heb. 11:21), was taken by John of Damascus (ca. 650), among others, to prefigure Christ hanging upon the axial Cross of the cosmos, raying out his blessings to the world.[16]

It is undoubtedly this strong connection of Jacob with the Axis that gave the ancient navigating and surveying device known as "Jacob's staff" its name. The Jacob's staff was basically a cross-staff along which the medieval navigator, surveyor, or geomancer would sight. This device may figure in a legend about the famous Salisbury Cathedral, also known as the Cathedral of St. Mary, whose building site is said to have been chosen by the flight of an arrow. It has been suggested that a Jacob's staff, which resembles a crossbow, may be behind the legend. According to this interpretation, the unlettered peasants would have mistaken the staff for a crossbow and then assumed the existence of an accompanying arrow. One must bear in mind, however, that the terms "arrow," "dart," and "spear" were commonly used during medieval times to designate forces that are, in the broadest sense of the word, "spiritual." Healing texts like the eleventh century *Lacnunga*,[17] for instance, speak of the elfin arrows or darts that bring illness, and Teresa of Avila describes a mystical experience wherein a fiery angel pierces her heart with a spear of love.[18] We note here that the English words "spear" and "spire" are virtually identical and that the French word for arrow, *fleche*, also refers to a church spire. In other words, the legend of the siting of Salisbury Cathedral by an arrow may have much to do with the axial energies available in the landscape.

The symbolism of the arrow and spear draws in other images of "piercing" and "transfixing." According to Gregory of Elvira (writing ca. 350), the magical staff with which Moses struck the rock bringing forth the gushing stream of the waters of life is the prototype of the Lance of Longinus that pierced the side of Christ, releasing the redemptive blood and water into the world.[19] We here touch again upon a version of the magical "history" of the sacred wood of the Paradisal Tree, in this case, closely allied with the waters of life, which themselves hearken back to the four rivers of paradise. And again too, the themes of regeneration and redemption appear. But with regard to the lance and its corollary the sword, we enter an enormously rich area of esoteric Christian symbolism and experience.

Of the many dragon-fighting legends in Christian tradition, those of Saint George and the Archangel Michael are undoubtedly the most important and the most widely dispersed in lore and iconography. These two may, in fact, be taken to represent two aspects or developments of a single esoteric motif.

The legend of Saint George is itself comprised of two main mythic components—the dragon fight and the martyrdom—both of which have important esoteric implications and structures. We are here concerned, though, with George the dragon slayer who according to legend was riding one day in the Cappadocian province of Libya where he came upon Sylene, a city being terrorized by a dragon.

The countryside surrounding the city had been all "envenomed" and was now a wasteland. Moreover, the citizens had begun sacrificing maidens to appease the dragon. When George arrived the chosen victim happened to be the King's daughter, who "had gone forth dressed as a bride to meet her doom." Saint George, however, transfixed the dragon with his lance and overthrew it. Then, using the maiden's garter as a harness, he led the beast back to the city. Many of the inhabitants of Sylene were baptized. Saint George then killed the dragon with his sword and ordered its body carried out into the surrounding fields in four wagons. And the land became fruitful and rich once again.[20]

Let us consider, first of all, how the presence of the dragon turns the countryside into a wasteland. The dragon in this case represents a manifestation of, or regression to, a fixed, chaotic state, a mode of existence where all is pure potency, undefined, and merely latent—all is in a perpetual state of winter. The first action required for the healing of the land is the transfixing of the dragon by the axial weapon. In most paintings, statues, and icons it is the head of the dragon which is pierced by the sword or lance.

We might recall here that according to certain rites of construction in India, at the place where the foundation stone for a building will be laid, the master mason drives a stake into the ground in order that the head of the earth serpent may be firmly fixed. In the legend of Saint George we see that the dragon is dispatched after the baptismal (that is, initiatory) rites take place.

Indeed, in early Christian ritual the descent into the water was closely linked to the fight with the dragon, just as the rising forth from the water was associated with the ascent of Jacob's Ladder.[21]

We are dealing then, in the legend of Saint George, with an initiatory scenario that affects and functions on both individual human and terrestrial environmental levels. For the land is regenerated by the cutting up and sowing of the dragon's parts in all the quarters of the region: Chaos is transformed into cosmos, ordered and manifested. The exemplary myth for this sequence is the slaying by God of the primordial dragon whose body is cut up to form the universe.[22] The initiatory pattern of death and rebirth, of descent and ascent, contained in the Saint George legend and enacted on a spiritual plane in the ancient baptismal rites thus echoes and is founded upon a primordial creative act of God.

The special relationship between the primal generation of the cosmos and the spiritual regeneration of the initiate reflects also a metaphysical tension that exists between a human being and his surroundings. The redemption of the fourfold elemental structure of the soul has immediate and direct effects on the environment in which that soul resides, and vice versa.

This theme has parallels in certain Grail legends. In particular, we refer to the tales of the dolorous stroke that laid the land to waste until it could be restored by one of purest heart and noble spirit. The dolorous stroke was brought about by the misuse of the Lance, that is, of the powers of the Axis, and this misuse resulted in the wounding of the "king" and the wasting of his realm. The key to the restoration of the broken realm lay in reestablishing the correct relationship between the Lance and the Grail, which, in the sense we are interested in, means the relationship between the Axis and the Center. In light of what has already been said regarding the role of the serpent's head in the fixing of the earth forces, we note that the Grail itself, in some versions of the legend, appears as a bleeding head.[23] Need we mention here that Christ is called "the Head" by the early church, or recall the bloody image of the crown of thorns?

Much of what we have been saying with regard to Saint George, the primordial creative act, initiation, the Grail legends, and so on is reiterated with a somewhat different emphasis in certain traditions which have grown up around the Archangel Michael.

In the Book of Revelation, for instance, Michael's defeat of the dragon is linked to events on a cosmic, apocalyptic plane that result in the utter transformation of the created order. At the risk of sounding self-contradictory, we might say that at very high degrees of spiritual understanding and esoteric experience, all intermediary degrees, planes, and worlds are abolished and a direct link is achieved between human consciousness and Divine Being. To an extent, the seven-headed dragon correlates with the seven heavens and spheres of being as articulated in traditional cosmology and anthropology. Michael, the wielder of the axial lance or sword, who chases the dragon out of heaven, thus becomes the agent of a mystical transformation.

Furthermore, it is this function as enabler of the interchange of spiritual energies between the Three Realms that accounts for why Saint Michael is considered the patron of so many sacred sites. Michael is particularly associated with those types of geographical features, such as certain hilltops, springs, and caves, that in a symbolic landscape are perceived as nodes or centers where ingress and egress to other realms and powers may be gained. We note finally the iconographical assimilation of the axial spear of the archangel to the axial cross of Christ so often seen in depictions of Michael fighting the dragon.

These few pages represent barely a fragment of the immense file dealing with the complex and important symbolism of the Cosmic Axis. We have, however, dug deep enough to at least begin to see the practical ramifications of the axial symbolism. A very general overview of the Axis, then, reveals three primary characteristics of immediate importance:

1. The Axis is a vertical channel or pivotal line that joins, transfixes, and binds the Three Realms. It is thus symbolically the "spindle" of creation around which the whole cosmic order revolves.

2. The Axis, especially as it is expressed in certain images such as the Tree, Ladder, Cross, or Body of Christ, functions as a *via sancta*, a holy way, often providing a very specific itinerary for the initiate's passage between the Three Realms and the Planes of Being.

3. The Axis likewise functions as a conduit through which spiritual energies flow between the Realms and Planes.

An exploration of the experiential significance of this triad of axial structures is undertaken in the practical work that follows.

VISION EXERCISE — CD Track 3

The Lance of Light

Using the kenosis meditation, enter the deep peace.

Begin to recite the ritual phrase for the Sphere of Creation exercise and, as you do this, be aware of the sphere of light building around you. The sphere expands, its light separating until you are aware of innumerable stars flashing upon the great indigo globe of the heavens. The landscape solidifies: You are standing upon the summit of a great mountain, and you are aware of the stream flowing nearby.

In the distance you see starlight glinting off the surface of a great sea. Looking toward the horizon, you become aware of a rising star. Following the movement of this star, you raise your vision until you gaze upon the pole star high above. And, as you meditate upon this pivotal point, you are suddenly aware of a ray of light shooting forth from it, descending with lightning speed to envelope you in a mighty pillar of light.

The pillar passes through the very center of the earth until it stretches from one pole of the cosmos to the other.

You are aware of yourself within this luminous column and find your spiritual vision is heightened.

You become aware of the great cosmic dance, of subtle currents of spiritual force at play within the universe and of the hierarchy of spiritual beings. You are conscious of petals of rainbow light descending—like manna from heaven—within the column toward you. Some of the petals pass within you, providing nourishment for your soul. Others move by you and disappear into the depths below.

You allow your gaze to follow them and perceive the crystals within the earth. As you gaze upon the shining gemstones beneath you, you are reminded of the lights of the stars above—to which you now return your attention. The landscape fades from vision. The sphere contracts, drawing the stars closer together into a bright orb of pure starlight. The axis grows thinner too, until it is as a narrow spear of infinite length running through the poles of the aura-sized orb surrounding you. You are in effect, "transfixed" by a lance of light passing through your spinal column. You meditate upon this, chanting to yourself the ritual phrase you have chosen (suggestions: "a piercing ray of deepest peace," "blessed are those transfixed by peace," or "be hallowed by a piercing ray").

3

The ḤOLY FIRE

he great German Theosopher Jacob Boehme wrote that at the creation of the universe "the unchangeable God moved himself toward fire and light and stirred up the fire-property."[1] More than two thousand years earlier, Heraclitus of Ephesus also spoke of fire as the primal element of the cosmos.[2] In Norse mythology, the fire giant Surt wields his flaming sword at the beginning and end of all creation.[3]

Indeed, many divine beings are closely associated with fire. The Hindu god Agni, for example, has flaming hair and, being reborn every time a new fire is kindled, remains eternally young.[4] In the Bhagavad Gita, Krishna is described as "flaming all around."[5] In Old Testament tradition, God appeared to Moses in the form of a burning bush (Exod. 3:21). During the dedication of Solomon's Temple, "fire came down from heaven . . . and the glory of the Lord filled the temple" (2 Chron. 7:1). The Dirghanana Sutra relates how once when the Buddha meditated in a cave the place was illumined by his "fiery ecstasy."[6] In the Dighanikaya we read that as the Buddha finished a discourse at Amaravati he said, "I have become a flame."[7] And according to the Gospel of Thomas, Jesus said, "Who is near me is near the fire."[8]

As this brief but varied glimpse into world traditions suggests, the symbolism of fire is complex and wide-ranging. It is far beyond the scope of this chapter to deal with the many details that make up the enormous dossier on sacred fire. We shall, therefore, confine our comments to a few themes that are likely to be of immediate practical value. Our aims are to outline, in general, the significance of the holy fire in Magical Christianity and to highlight certain features of what might be called "Christian *kundalini*," as it involves the invocation or arousal of the divine fire within the initiate.

As always, whenever we seek the deeper issues of esotericism, we find ourselves immersed in traditional lore. In a legend collected in Persia by Marco Polo,[9] fire is connected with a magical stone given the Three Magi after they brought the myrrh, frankincense and gold to the Christ Child at Bethlehem. According to this story the Magi received, in exchange for their gifts, a small casket containing a stone. On their journey home they cast the stone into a well of immense depth and immediately fire descended from heaven into that well, then roared up in a blaze that lit the sky. The Magi were amazed. Aware that here was something great and holy, they took a spark of the fire and brought it back to their own country. There, inside a magnificent church, the fire was kept perpetually burning.

This simple legend has several layers of esoteric significance. Note the presence of the four elements: *earth*, represented by the stone; *water*, by the well; *air*, the medium through which the *fire* passes; and *fire* itself. The fire originates in the Celestial Region. Its path of descent traces the line of the World Axis.

In fact, one of the symbolic functions of the well is to complete the line of the Axis by being the channel through which the holy fire passes into the UnderEarth, thereby conjoining it with the Celestial and Terrestrial Regions. There is, then, a representation not only of the four elements, that is, the essential constituents and root qualities of creation, but also of the Three Realms or Regions that define the cosmos in a vertical plane.

Furthermore, there is a precise relationship between the fire and the stone. In addition to being an image of the element of earth, the stone represents a cosmic center, or rather *the* Cosmic Center, the heart of the mystical body of Christ. The divine fire with its origins in the realm of the heavens and its destination at the Cosmic Center brings about the fusion of all beings, realms, worlds, elements, powers, and energies. All are united within the Center, all are infused with the living fire of the Holy Spirit.

In our next chapter we shall see how the Cosmic Center, the "heart of God," and the human heart are linked through a series of symbolic resonances. For the moment, however, let us mark the close relationship between the holy fire and the heart—a relationship that depends in part upon the shared symbolism of spiritual love. The English hermit Richard Rolle writes of his experience of the inner fire in the *Incendium Amoris*:

> I cannot tell you how surprised I was the first time I felt my heart begin to warm. It was a real warmth too, not imaginary, and it felt as if it were actually on fire. . . . I had to keep feeling my breast to make sure there was no physical reason for it! But once I realized it came entirely from within, that this fire of love had no cause, material or sinful but was the gift of my Maker, I was absolutely delighted, and wanted my love to be even greater. . . . It set my soul aglow as if a real fire was burning there.[10]

Meister Eckhart, in a powerful passage, also writes of fiery love, but as a force that suffused the cosmos at the Crucifixion: "On the Cross his Heart burnt like a fire and a furnace from which the flame burst forth on all sides. So was he inflamed on the Cross by his fire of love for the whole world."[11] The perspectives represented by these two authors—the personal and the universal—are quite complementary. For as we shall repeatedly see, the arousal of the holy fire within the initiate amounts to nothing less than an *imitatio Christi*.

But the fire of divine love is also the fire of holy wisdom: "And he gave me a goblet filled with fire, and when I had drunk it wisdom grew in me. . . ," says an apocryphal book of Ezra.[12] There is a legend in which Saint Thomas touches the wound in the side of Christ (i.e., the heart) and draws forth fire.[13] Thomas is, of course, the great "gnostic," the one who sought direct knowledge of the divine wisdom, and the one who came to know it by touching the fiery heart of Christ.

Fire as a symbol of the direct transmission of holy wisdom is one of the initiatory keys of Magical Christianity. To the prepared soul the experience of the *hagia sophia* brings, among much else, a direct knowledge of the relatedness of all things. In the tradition of Pentecost, when the divine fire rests upon the Apostles, they are able to speak to any man in any tongue (Acts 2:1–11). In other words, the spiritual barriers of separation are removed and they realize their relatedness to all beings. They are given a glimpse of the primordial wholeness. In specific mythological terms they are returned to the golden age before the confusion of tongues (Gen. 11:1).

To know a thing spiritually, then, is to realize one's profound relatedness to it, *substantialis*, and thereby, through the harmonic quality of consciousness, to realize one's relatedness to the totality of cosmos and Creator. This experience places the mage in the role of mediator, capable, if willing, of acting as a channel for divine energies, for mediation is a direct outcome of attunement with spiritual reality.

Several of the methods used to tune consciousness in the Western mysteries today are, in fact, modifications of techniques well known in certain early Christian circles. The deliberate and conscious development, purification, and transformation of one's soul through the agency of divine fire, the *ignis invisibilis et spiritualis*, is fairly well evidenced, for one, in the legends and visions of the Egyptian Desert Fathers:

> Once, a monk went to see the hermit Abba Joseph and said, "Abba, according to my means I have accomplished my humble service, my humble fasting, my prayer, my meditation and my seclusion, according to my means I try to be pure in my thought. What more can I do?" Then Joseph stood up and spread his hands toward Heaven. His fingers became like ten flames of fire. And he said: "If you want to, you can become wholly like fire."[14]

On another occasion, a brother traveled to the cell of Abba Arsenius in the desert. When he arrived outside the door, he looked in the window and saw the old man as a great flame of fire.[15]

One day Mark the Egyptian was offering up a prayer at Mass when he had a vision. An angel of the Lord descended from heaven and placed his hand upon the head of the presiding priest, who became as a burning column of fire.[16]

Another desert monk, Constantine of Bethany, was reciting a psalm at Matins when his appearance was transformed into a great pillar of fire.[17]

The experience of the divine fire was not limited to individuals alone. According to *The Paradise of the Fathers*, when monks gathered to pray, they generated a column of fire that reached to heaven.[18]

As these accounts suggest, the holy fire represents not only the descent of spiritual power, but also the means of ascent or attunement to the divine presence. "Not only is the Godhead brought down to man, but man is raised up to the Godhead." It will be observed that several of our examples focus on the image of a column or pillar of fire. In these instances the image of divine fire also functions as a symbol of the Universal Axis, which, as we have said, is the channel through which spiritual energy moves between the Realms. Thus it is that columns and pillars have a particular significance in the founding and integral structure of many ancient churches.

An Armenian legend of Saint Nino tells what happened after the king's builders failed numerous times to erect the pillar for a new church:

St. Nino accompanied by twelve women from among her disciples remained by the column and wept. Then Nino arose and stretched out her arms in prayer to God, and said, "May this project on which the king is engaged not be brought to nothing." When dawn approached, the women fell asleep, but Nino stood with upraised hands. Suddenly there appeared by her a young man adorned with brilliant light and shrouded in fire. He spoke three words to her, at which she fell down upon her face. Then the youth touched the pillar with his hand and raised it, and it stood up. And the pillar blazed like a column of fire, and moved by itself to approach its base. There it stood twelve cubits above its pedestal, which had been carved for it out of the stump of that same cedar tree from which this Living Pillar was hewn out.

At dawn the king got up in a mood of depression, and went to look at the garden and at the church which he had started to build with so much enthusiasm. Shooting up towards heaven from his garden he saw a light like a flash of lightning. He came running to the spot with all his followers and the townspeople who had also observed the marvel. Then the column, resplendent with light, descended on to its place as if from heaven, and stood firmly on its base without being touched by human hands.[19]

The legend refers to a fiery "living pillar" as the core and support of the holy edifice. In accordance with the esoteric doctrine of correspondences, ancient churches often replicate symbolically both the cosmic structure and the human constitution: body, soul, and spirit. There is, then, an esoteric formula underpinning the legend of Saint Nino that might be summarized as follows: World Axis = Cosmic Tree (Sacred Tree) = fiery pillar of church = spinal column. The living pillar of fire, consecrated by the touch of the flame-being—here an angel or even possibly Christ—enables the building, and by extension the human being, to exist as a sacred site, a place where holy presence is manifest.

Let us also recall that angels are typically described as fiery beings. The foundational pillar or column of fire may thus also represent an angelic presence overseeing the sacred site. Here we have a glimpse into the reality behind the popular traditions of guardian or guiding angels, for these holy beings were probably originally associated with sacred places rather than with particular individual souls. This allows, of course, that an individual would have come under the protection and direction of the angelic presence associated with his or her place of worship.

The pillar of fire is an image that occurs in Christian mystical and magical tradition with some frequency. In Christian mythology it finds its prototype in the Old Testament story of Exodus. The Israelites are guided into the promised land by a pillar of cloud during the day and a pillar of fire at night. Both these images came fairly early on to denote, interchangeably, the mystical ascent of the soul to God and the descent of divine *energia* into the soul.

Over time the images came to signify two distinct, even opposing, approaches to mystical experience. The pillar of cloud became a root image—and this is somewhat paradoxical—for the *via negativa*, the way of negation, in which the soul rejects all images and attributes in its quest for God. (The method is aptly described in an anonymous medieval manual titled *The Cloud of Unknowing*.) The pillar of fire, on the other hand, became a key symbol for the *via affirmativa*, that is, the way of affirmation, in which the soul seeks God through images and attributes.

Our concern at present, however, is less with mysticism (i.e., the quest for personal union with God) than it is with becoming a channel for the work of God, with becoming a mediator of spiritual energy to the world at large, with what Dionysios the Areopagite and others term "theurgy."

Dionysios's writings date from the sixth century, but the tradition he represents dates from the time of Paul.[20]

Dionysios is considered the great spokesman for the *via negativa*. To be sure, he was the first Christian adept to write extensively of the divine darkness and the unknowability of God, but he also ably articulated a "metaphysics of light,"[21] and his works are filled with profound exegeses of symbols. Dionysios was well aware that the "promised land" was reached by following *both* the pillar of cloud *and* the pillar of fire. Dionysios says of fire: "The Word of God seems to honor the depiction of fire above all others. You will find that it depicts not only flaming wheels, but also burning animals and even men who are somehow aglow."[22]

In writing of "men who are somehow aglow," Dionysios is drawing attention to long-standing traditions of the awakening of the holy fire within the Christian initiate. Elsewhere, he writes that "the power of fire causes a lifting up to the godlike."[23]

We have seen that the desert monks sought to attain the fiery state of illumination through ascetic practice. Yet the possibility of illumination, as a *hic et nunc* experience, is itself fully present in the initiation rites—particularly before the church suppressed its own arcane disciplines. The rituals of illumination are mentioned in ancient texts in connection with several symbolic terms and images that are of interest to us here.

At least as early as the fourth century, inner visions relating to the descent and ascent of spiritual luminescence were deliberately induced during the initiation rites. A baptismal hymn written by Ephram the Syrian contains the following lines:

> O brothers, open your senses and contemplate
> the hidden column,
> whose base rests upon the waters
> and which rises to the celestial gate,
> like the ladder that Jacob saw.
> On it the light descends to the baptism,
> and the soul rises to heaven,
> so that all may be united in love.[24]

More detailed descriptions of the symbolism involved in the ancient initiatory visions are to be found embedded in the lives of certain saints. *The Acts of St. Marina*, for instance, also dating from the fourth century, contains some interesting elements.

One episode in particular, tells how Saint Marina, having been condemned to die by drowning, prayed that her chains be broken and that the water serve as her sanctification and initiation into the baptismal mystery. Then she addressed the Risen Christ, saying, "O eternal one, may you envelop me with your spirit, with your holy garment." And straightaway there descended from heaven a dove bearing a crown in its beak. Then the chains of the saint fell away as she stood up in the water, praising and glorifying God. The dove darted quickly to Marina and touched her lightly and said to her, "Peace be with you, servant of Jesus. Take heart, for in this moment you are to be crowned." The dove extended its wings and flew out of the water. And a column of fire appeared from heaven, and above it was a cross.

Marina gave thanks and exclaimed, "The Lord is become my king, he is shrouded in beautiful garments. You are my illumination, Jesus Christ, O Rabbi, Adonai, I have been freed by the light of the Lord. You have glorified me, Lord Jesus, you have justified me, Christ, and you have clothed me with your holy vestment."[25]

The story of Marina's experience accords with what we know of the ancient rites. Not only is the central theme one of liberation or salvation, but in terms of the actual rubrics of baptism, we know that candidates were crowned and received new vestments in the form of white robes (white symbolizing light, purity, illumination, and other qualities characterized by sacred fire).[26]

Let us also recall that the baptized were often known as *illuminati* and that their experience of illumination was undoubtedly bound up with the consonant symbolism of water and fire.[27]

John Climacus reveals an awareness of the occult connection between these two elements when he remarks how those who have attained to the "angelic state" become "incorruptible"—they no longer desire food and cannot become sick—because they are "sustained by a celestial fire" that is just like "an underground stream that nourishes the root of a plant."[28]

According to Persian tradition, *xavarenah*, the vital fire or radiance that pervades and enables all life, rises through the medium of water into all animals, plants, and humans. In the latter it is said to concentrate in the head, from whence it radiates a glowing light. This is the origin of the nimbus, or halo, that shines about the heads of the saints.[29]

The correlation between the holy fire and the "angelic state" of illumination also figures strongly in the legend of the martyrdom of Theodorus. According to this tradition the saint had a vision of a ladder that rose from the depths of the earth to the heights of heaven. An enormous dragon lived at the foot of the ladder. At the top was a mighty figure sitting on a magnificent throne, around which were a myriad of flaming beings. The one who was seated on the throne said to Theodorus, "Do you want to be my child?" Theodorus said, "Who are you, Lord?" "I am Jesus the Logos of God; your blood will be soon spilled in my name." Then Theodorus was lifted up and baptized with the baptism of fire. He was taken to the Lake of Fire and plunged in three times; and he became wholly of fire like those who are gathered about the throne.[30]

This vision, occurring just before his martyrdom, was given in preparation for Theodorus's entry to the Celestial Realm. It contains three key symbols or motifs: the ladder, the dragon, and the baptism by fire. The ladder as it relates to the Cosmic Axis, the Cross, and the mystical body of Christ has been treated in the previous chapter. The symbol of the dragon and its corollary the serpent we have also looked at from the perspective of cosmic transformation. There is however another less well known, and certainly esoteric, aspect to the figure of the serpent or dragon—its role as a symbol of the Axis itself.

There is a Jewish midrash (Berashith Rabba 68), for instance, which identifies the dragon with Jacob's Ladder, by way of which the angels ascend and descend to rescue the souls of the dead.

The New Testament assigns the symbol of the fiery serpent to Christ himself: "And as Moses lifted up the serpent in the wilderness, so must the Son of Man be lifted up"(John 3:14). The serpent that Moses lifted up refers to an Old Testament story that relates how the Israelites were attacked by fiery serpents. "So Moses prayed for the people. And the Lord said to Moses, 'Make a fiery serpent, and set it on a pole; and every one who is bitten, when he sees it, shall live'" (Num. 21:4–9).

In practical esoteric terms the fiery serpent/dragon force must be "crucified," raised up, that it may open the higher modes of awareness, enabling the initiate to perceive directly the nature of spiritual reality.

An alternative model for this process is the baptism of fire. After Theodorus is immersed thrice in the Lake of Fire, he becomes "wholly of fire" like the angels about the throne. Esoterically speaking, the threefold immersion represents, inter alia, the candidate's initiation into the mysteries of the Three Cosmic Regions; his passage through the three "ages of man"—a symbolic completion of the rounds of birth and death; and his ritual enactment of the three days of Christ in the tomb preceding the Resurrection.

According to Dionysios's *Celestial Hierarchy*, the angels nearest the divine throne or Center are the *seraphim*. This is the word translated as "fiery serpents" in the passage from Numbers quoted above.

Dionysios translates the word as both "those who are on fire" and "makers of fire." In the Dionysian tradition the term *seraphim* designates on one hand the fiery nature of the angelic beings themselves and on the other, their power to illuminate others.[31] The purpose of the baptism of fire, then, is to transmute the soul by raising it to an angelic vibration. It signifies both a mystical and personally transformative vision and also the awakening and arousal within the initiate of the capacity to mediate the holy power of illumination.

The baptism of fire is a motif found frequently in the ancient visions, and invariably takes place in either a lake or river of fire. Occasionally, as in the Apocalypse of Bartholomew, the two images of fiery lake and flaming river occur together.

According to this legend, the Apostle Thomas revived his son Siophanes, who had lain dead for seven days. Siophanes then related how his soul had journeyed through the heavens under the conduct of the Archangel Michael. He was led through the celestial regions with the angels singing before him. They came to a river of fire, and Michael took him by the hand and led him into the river, whereupon Siophanes became like a flaming fire. Afterwards the archangel brought him to a lake of fire and immersed him three times in its waters. Then a voice sounded out of the heights bidding the angels to conduct him to the celestial paradise.[32]

From the point of view of esoteric function, the lake of fire and the river of fire are synonymous images—as are their biblical prototypes, the Red Sea and the Jordan River. In the Old Testament, the crossing of the Red Sea and the crossing of the Jordan River both constitute liberation from an oppressive or unfulfilled mode of existence. It is partly for this reason that these myths were invoked during the Christian rituals as paradigms of initiation. More importantly, the crossing of the Red Sea and the crossing of the Jordan were invoked during the rites because they were also symbolically resonant with Jesus's own baptism in the Jordan.

We need hardly reiterate here the importance of the baptism of Christ as a *leitmotif* in the early initiation ceremonies. What is worth noting, however, is the existence of several ancient references clearly linking the baptism in the Jordan with holy fire. In the second century, for example, Justin wrote, "When Jesus had descended into the water, the Jordan was set on fire."[33] When touched by Divine Being, elemental water is transformed into spiritual fire. The fiery river and lake might thus be termed the spiritual octaves of the Jordan and the Red Sea. They sound the same notes on a higher level.

As the tales of Theodorus and Siophanes show, the baptism of fire is an experience of profound purification and transformation that prepares one for the knowledge of the upper realms, the celestial hierarchy, and the stages of being leading to the Godhead.

It is, in short, the higher octave of the baptism of water and constitutes an initiation within the initiation, reserved for those able and willing to receive it.

Furthermore, the arousal within the initiate of the holy fire, the purpose of which is the attainment or awakening of the "resurrection body" is firmly based upon an exemplary pattern laid down by Christ's baptism in the Jordan. Origen puts it succinctly thus: "In the baptism of water, we are entombed with Christ; in the baptism of fire, we are configured to his glorious body."[34] Here we are reminded of the legend of Saint Marina and how the Christ appeared to her vested in fire. But other traditions are even more explicit.

In his chapter entitled "The Mystery of Illumination," Dionysios remarks how Christ descended "like a fire," making "one with himself all those capable of being divinized."[35] James of Sarug (500) says, "How marvelous and astonishing it is to relate how the fire, enveloped in a body, was baptized in the water and how the high flame-being... descended into the Jordan to be laved."[36] Finally, a Syrian text describes the moment of Jesus' baptism as follows: "There is a spark in the water, a flame glideth up and down in the wave. God is being laved in the Jordan."[37]

It is precisely because the Christ takes the form of fire that the initiate seeks to arouse the holy fire within himself. By becoming attuned to the spiritual symbolism of fire, one becomes attuned to Universal Being, and to the flow of divine love, wisdom, and power between the Realms. One thus becomes capable—especially if skilled in the use of intercessory ritual, prayer, and meditation—of acting as a channel for archetypal energies (figure 6).[38]

Training in a mystery school aims at bringing out latent talents and abilities to be used in service to the inner orders of saints and adepts under the Living Son of Light. Since the occult energies that

Figure 6.
The "Gifts of the Spirit"

The "gifts of the Spirit" are usually numbered seven. These may be subdivided into two groups of three, with the gift of Piety (spiritual conduct) as the working out of the other gifts on the physical plane. Love, Wisdom, and Power thus constitute the Greater Triad; counsel, knowledge, and awe comprise the Lesser Triad. In this illustration, the seven gifts are shown in the context of the seven centers of occult and mystical physiology. These spiritual centers have (somewhat fluid) connections to certain organs and regions of the physical body, in this case, the crown, throat, heart, solar plexus, navel, genitals, and feet.

are embodied in the image of fire are by nature creative, magical forces emanating from Divine Being and residing in the cosmos and the soul, their arousal can result in the manifestation of certain psychic phenomena, or in the awakening in the individual of gifts, virtues, and powers. As attested in all the esoteric traditions, such an awakening may also entail some temporary emotional turbulence as the newly released inner energies find their level—though this is minimized by dedication to a higher cause. The exercise that follows is quite safe, therefore, if undertaken with the intention of arousing one's potential for use in service to Divine Being, and if kept within the context of the entire series of exercises given in this book.

VISION EXERCISE ⌣ CD Track 4

The Living Flame

*H*aving performed the kenosis meditation, begin to recite the *ceremonial phrase for the Sphere of Creation. As you do this, be aware of a luminous sphere building around you.*

Feel the sphere expanding. And as the sphere grows, its light separates into innumerable points that flash as stars upon the indigo darkness of the celestial orb.

The landscape forms about you. You stand upon the plateau at the summit of the mountain. Near you runs the stream and in the distance you catch the glint of starlight on the surface of a great sea.

Next, recite the phrase for the Lance of Light and become aware of the axis of light running through the poles of the sphere and through the line of your spinal column.

Be aware of the crystals within the earth and of their celestial counterparts, the stars above.

Now reach your consciousness upwards, beyond the pole of the cosmic sphere, up towards the source of absolute illumination.

Become aware, out of this infinite light, of the figure of a dove descending towards you along the line of the axis of light. The dove gradually assumes the form of a river of golden fire. And the fire shoots down, passing through your spinal column like a rushing wind or waterfall.

Having descended deep into the heart of the earth, it kindles there a secret spiritual flame. The stream of fire then turns back and slowly begins to rise up the shaft of the axis towards you. It enters the base of your spinal column and rushes up to your head, flowing into your cranium, filling your mind with bright, golden fire.

You feel your head transformed into a blazing disk of light with tongues of flame shooting upward from it like the peaks of a crown.

A shower of golden sparks now begins to fall from your head, forming a pool of golden light at your feet. This rises about you in a great tide. You are immersed in a wondrous sea of golden fire.

This sea of light gradually fades. And you become aware that your entire body has become transfigured into a golden flame of divine spirit.

The fire recedes, slowly emptying through your feet, then moves back down the axis. The fire briefly merges with the flame at the center of the earth, whereupon the crystals within the land flash momentarily like a blanket of stars. The stream of living fire passes through the earth. As it nears the opposite pole of the cosmos, it resumes the form of a white dove and is once again received into the light of the Absolute.

The sphere contracts, drawing the stars together until they merge again into one sphere of pure starlight. And you are aware also of the lance of infinite length running through your spinal column and through the poles of the aura-sized sphere by which you are encompassed.

And still glowing, deep within the cave of your heart is a bright spark of the golden fire brought by the dove of spirit. You meditate upon the significance of this living flame.

And as you do so, you repeat to yourself the ceremonial phrase you have chosen (suggestions: "a holy fount of living fire," "blessed are those who raise up the fire," or "be hallowed by a living fire").

CHAPTER FOUR

The CENTER

ost traditional cultures claim one or more sacred sites as marking a central "heart" or "navel" of the world. For the Kogi of northwestern Colombia, for instance, the entire range of the Sierra Nevada is located at the heart of the cosmos. Not only collectively, but also individually, the mountains are seen to give access to the Center. Man was born on the summit of a mountain and to this place of origin his soul returns at death. Moreover, the mountains are perceived as reflecting the very structure of the universe, and this structure is in turn mirrored in the architecture of the ceremonial lodge. Each lodge is marked by openings to the four directions, and from the midpoint of the conical roof hangs a thread that connects the peak to the navel of the Earth Mother. The Kogi also encounter the Mother in caves representing the cosmic womb.[1]

I mentioned earlier (chapter 1) a connection between the ceremonial *kivas* of the Pueblo Indians of New Mexico and the cosmic womb. In the Tewa Pueblo of San Juan, there exists a circle of stones known as the "earth mother earth navel middle place." Though now located in the south plaza, the Earth Mother Navel was at one time located inside a circular *kiva*. This central navel is both the place of origin and the source for continued life. It is from here the people first emerged into this world. Here too is the source of "blessings" which radiate outward across the land. The blessings are gathered in by a set of secondary earth navels (also composed of stones, but shaped like keyholes or open wombs) on the four sacred mountains and redirected towards the various Tewa villages. Furthermore, all the earth navels in the Tewa cosmos are points of intersection between the Three Cosmic Regions (over, under, and middle).[2]

What is useful about our knowledge of the Kogi and Tewa worlds is that they demonstrate the function and structure of the Center within the context of a complete symbolic cosmos. Human and divine beings, architecture, and the sacred landscape all have intense correlations, all are entwined in a set of meaningful relations through their connection to the Center. It is obvious we are dealing with notions that are extremely ancient and widespread and have their basis in a perception of the cosmos as the "garment" of the sacred. Certain features in the landscape are capable of revealing or giving access to the deeper or higher mysteries of being and creation. In almost every tradition, the Center is associated with a sacred mountain, tree, stone, spring, or cave.

In Taoist tradition, the World Mountain, *k'un-lun*, is some three thousand miles high. There may be found the fountain of immortality and from there flow the four great world rivers. Its slopes are of gold and silver and precious stones, and on it, at the center of the universe, reside the Four Kings of Heaven.[3]

In Christian lore, paradise, "the place where the earth joins the sky,"[4] is an inaccessible garden surrounded by a fiery wall that reaches to the heavens. "Here is the tree of life which gives immortality, here is the fountain which divides into four streams that go forth to water the world."[5] Christian tradition also often places paradise on a mountain. For Godfrey of Viterbo (1186), for example, paradise is "a golden mountain redolent with wonderful odors and adorned with an image of Virgin and Child."[6]

In Dante's *Divine Comedy*, the earthly paradise is located upon the peak of Mount Purgatory. This peak is formed of earth that, before being displaced as a result of the Fall, was originally at the exact center of the terrestrial orb.[7]

For the Samaritans, Gerizim is known as *eres tabbur*, "the navel of the earth." It is the holy mountain where God created Adam, where Noah landed in his ark, where Isaac was bound by Abraham, where Jacob dreamed of his ladder and set up a sacred stone, where patriarchs are buried, and where Moses looked as he lay dying nearby.[8]

In the Book of Jubilees (8:19) we are told that "the Garden of Eden is the holy of holies, and the dwelling of the Lord, and Mount Sinai the center of the desert and Mount Zion the center of the navel of the earth. . . ." These two mountains, Sinai and Zion (Mount Moriah), represented for the ancient Israelites places where the center of the universe could be found. In pre-Davidic times, Sinai was the pre-eminent node, for it was where Yahweh gave the Law to Moses. After the establishment of Jerusalem as the capital of the kingdom, the divine presence at Mount Sinai became accessible at Mount Zion, and Zion assumed many of the attributes of Sinai.[9]

In ancient Greece, the Center manifested in the form of a sacred stone known as the *omphalos* (literally, "navel"). Most important was the omphalos at the temple of Apollo at Delphi.[10] The site was determined when two eagles sent out by Zeus, one from the east, the other from the west, met at this spot. Alternatively, according to Peloponnesian myth, when the goddess Harmonia wove the fabric of the universe, "she first represented the earth with its omphalos in the center."[11]

The development of the traditions of the Foundation Stone at Jerusalem was influenced both by the Hellenistic conceptions of the omphalos and by the indigenous traditions of Palestine and Syria, where sacred stones were also numerous. Known as *baetyls* or *bethels*, there were famous examples at the Temple of El Gabel in Emesa and in a mountaintop shrine near Antioch, to name but two.[12] In the Old Testament the place where Jacob laid his head upon a stone and dreamed of a ladder reaching to heaven became known as *Bethel* (Gen. 28:11–19). The Foundation Stone itself was located at the site of the Holy of Holies in Solomon's Temple. Now housed by the Dome of the Rock, it consists of a roughly rectangular slab with a cave inside.

There is a whole assemblage of important symbols connected to the Foundation Stone: In Islamic tradition, at the end of time the *Kaaba* will fuse with the Foundation Stone.[13] Moreover, the cave within the stone, known as the "well of souls" is the place wherefrom Mohammed ascended to paradise.[14] According to Rabbinic tradition,

> Just as the navel is found at the center of a human being, so the land of Israel is found at the center of the world . . . and it is the foundation of the world. Jerusalem is at the center of the land of Israel, the Temple is at the center of Jerusalem, the Holy of Holies is at the center of the Temple, the Ark is at the center of the Holy of Holies and the Foundation Stone is in front of the Ark, which spot is the foundation of the world.[15]

Moreover, for the Israelites, the Foundation Stone is where Yahweh stood at the beginning of time, where Adam was created and buried, where Abraham shared in the mystic bread and wine with Melchizedek, where Jacob had his dream-vision. It is also the lid to the entrance to the UnderRealm and from it the primal light flowed at the creation.[16]

In the New Testament, Christ is connected to the traditions of the Foundation Stone when he is called the "chief cornerstone," the "living stone, . . . chosen and precious." And it is the loss of the Center that is being alluded to when Christ is referred to as the stone that the builders rejected (1 Pet. 2:1–7, Eph. 3:21–22, Acts 4:11).

Images of the Center abound in Christian lore. It is well known to biblical scholars that Jerusalem plays a central role in parts of the New Testament, especially the Lukan and Johannine writings. In Luke and Acts, Jerusalem is the central reference point. All the important events are placed in relation to Jerusalem.[17] In Luke, the movement is generally towards Jerusalem, that is, towards the place where the central sacred events will occur. In Acts, the movement is generally away from Jerusalem: the Apostles go forth into the world bearing with them the teaching and power originally bestowed upon them and periodically renewed for them at the heart of the world. In the Johannine writings, the emphasis is on the New Jerusalem—an imaginal symbol of the Center.

The relationship between the spiritual Center and its physical and imaginal symbols is of great import for esoteric Christian practice and requires at least a brief elaboration. It would be useful at this point, therefore, to underscore the distinction between the *Center* and the *nodes*. The Center is a spiritual reality. It is what Plato calls a divine idea or form, and what Philo and, later, Augustine refer to as an archetype. There is no one sacred site, symbol, or image that can contain or reveal the total power and significance of the Center. This is why there can be more than one place or image designated as the center of the world, even within the same tradition. The sites and symbols of the Center—whether they be physical places like Mount Gerizim, Jerusalem, and Golgotha or imaginal constructs like *k'un-lun*, the New Jerusalem, and the Sacred Heart of Jesus—are merely nodes, gateways giving access to something that is otherwise inaccessible.

Let us reiterate. The Center is neither primarily a geographic site nor a geometric point, but a spiritual principle. Though it may be accessed through specialized nodes in sacred landscapes (whether physical or imaginal) and though we may gain a circumstantial understanding of its significance through geometric symbolism, the Center must not be confused with these expressions.

The spiritual significance of the Center transcends its physical and imaginal manifestations. This is why early maps have a tendency to be diagrammatic and symbolic rather than literal and physically accurate. The physical imprecision is not due merely to a lack of geographic knowledge, but to participation in a symbolic cosmos, a world in which reality is gauged more by fullness of meaning and spiritual power than by quantitative measurement. Thus on many ancient European maps, Jerusalem is positioned at the center, not so much because it was considered the central point in the circle of a flat world, but because it was the most sacred place on earth.

A similar perspective might be assumed when we read the accounts of pilgrims to sacred sites. An Icelandic traveler, Nicholas of Thverva, made a pilgrimage to the Holy Land in the twelfth century. Of the Holy Sepulcher he wrote: "the center of the World is there; there, on the day of the summer solstice, the light of the sun falls perpendicularly from heaven."[18] But the sun doesn't actually fall straight down over the Sepulcher, for Jerusalem is about nine degrees north of the Tropic of Cancer.

Another pilgrim to Jerusalem, Melito of Sardis (ca. AD 160), insists that the site of Christ's crucifixion lay at the "center of the city."[19] Golgotha was in fact located just outside the walls of Jerusalem during the time of Christ, and it is in this location also that Melito would have viewed it in the second century.

There is probably neither ignorance, duplicity, nor delusion involved in these accounts. When powerful spiritual forces touch the soul, the physical world can be, and sometimes is, transfigured. The cosmos assumes a perfect form, one wholly in accord with the structure of spiritual reality. Far from being a hallucination or wishful daydream, this is rather a kind of deep spiritual vision. One sees things not only as they should be, but as they really are *in potentia*. Nicholas of Thverva may have really seen the sun shining perpendicularly at the solstice and Melito of Sardis may have actually perceived Golgotha to be at the center of Jerusalem.[20]

Whatever one's opinion of the experiences of Nicholas and Melito, however, the sites they visited, the mount of the Crucifixion, and the tomb of Christ, are both powerful nodes with highly developed traditions relating to the Center. Certain Christian legends place the tomb of Adam beneath the Mount of Golgotha. Origen was aware of these, as was Basil of Caesarea (d. 349). The latter remarks that the skull of Adam was hidden beneath the hill upon which Christ was crucified.[21] In the Syrian *Book of the Cave of Treasures*, we read that Adam was created and buried at the center of the earth, on the same site where the cross of Christ was later erected. As a result, Christ's blood fell upon the skull of the first man, redeeming him, and thus making redemption possible for all humanity. [22]

There is a kinship here with Paul's doctrine of Christ as the new Adam, the primal ancestor and exemplar who comes at the beginning of the new creation.

As remarked, Golgotha was not the only site to be seen as a world center by the Christians. Near it lay the Holy Sepulcher, the place where Christ was buried, where he descended to the UnderRealm, and whence he emerged resurrected. When Christianity was allowed public reclamation of its holy sites in Jerusalem in the fourth century, tradition dictated that the Lord was buried in a cave beneath what had long been a temple of the goddess Venus. It was this that became the site for the church of the Holy Sepulcher—a fact which serves to emphasize the concordance between the divine feminine and the Cosmic Center.

The sacred cave is, in and of itself, a symbol of the Center. As we have already noted, the cave is symbolic of the place of cosmic origins, the womb of creation. But it is also a place where access is gained to the Axis, and thus to all the Realms and Planes of Being.[23] The Holy Sepulcher was one of three sacred caves held most holy by the early Christians. The others were the Cave of the Nativity, and the rarely mentioned Cave of the Ascension. (It was, according to early traditions, from a cave near the summit of the Mount of Olives that Christ ascended.)[24]

This same cave appears in a somewhat different context in an apocryphal gospel of John. The text relates how during the time of the Crucifixion, John goes to the Mount of Olives and enters a cave. There he sees the figure of Christ standing before him, his very presence illuminating the darkness of the cave.

The Lord gives John a vision of a cross of light and speaks to him of its esoteric significance: "This cross . . . is that which joined all things unto itself by the word, . . . and then also, being one, made all things flow forth."[25] Here we have the images of the mountain, the Cross, and the cave occurring together. More importantly, note that the Cross is that which both unites and enables creation.

A number of other important documents mention this cosmic doctrine of the Cross. The *Clementine Homilies*, for example, speak of the creation as follows:

There proceeds from God, the heart of the world, indefinite extension—upwards and downwards, to the right and left, backward and forward. Looking in these six directions, as at a constant number, he completes the creation of the world, of which he is the beginning and the end. In him the six phases of time have their end, and it is from him that they receive their indefinite extension. And that is the secret of the number seven.[26]

In simple geometric terms, this passage demonstrates a set of cosmic relationships that are appropriately expressed in the symbol of the six-pointed cross so well known from early Christian inscriptions. This type of cross is also the underlying pattern for the *chi rho* or monogram of Christ (figure 7). It is a symbol that expresses creation as the development of a three-dimensional Cosmic Cross out of the divine center, "the heart of the world," as Clement calls it.

Figure 7.
Six-pointed cross and
monogram of Christ

The symbolism of the Cross as or at the Center is taken up from a different perspective in the Acts of Peter. Peter is crucified upside down in order to reverse the pattern of creation warped by the fall of Adam:

"Concerning which the Lord saith in a mystery: 'Unless ye make the things of the right hand as those of the left, and those of the left as those of the right, and those that are above as those below, and those that are behind as those that are before, ye shall not have knowledge of the kingdom.'"[27]

Peter then remarks that the nail or pivot at the center of the cross represents "conversion," that is, it signifies a true change of heart. Naturally, we are speaking not of a switch in allegiance to a particular creed or belief, but of a transformed vision of the cosmos and one's role in it as a spiritual being.

Several other traditions pend from or fill out the initiatory importance of the central Cosmic Cross. In some early commentaries, for instance, baptism is explicitly linked both to the cross of Christ (and thus Golgotha) and to his burial (and thus the Holy Sepulcher): "Baptism is a cross," writes John Chrysostom. "What the Cross was to Christ and what His burial was, that baptism was to us."[28] And Ambrose says that when baptism occurs "you take on the likeness of death and burial; you receive the sacrament of the Cross."[29] It is not really surprising that references to these two primary nodes should appear in connection with the rites of initiation. For the initiatory experience is always in some form a return to the Source, a death and rebirth occurring at the center of creation and existence.

Golgotha and the Holy Sepulcher are also particularly linked to the figure of Joseph of Arimathea. In the New Testament, the body of Christ is given into Joseph's care to be properly prepared for burial in the tomb.

Later apocryphal works provide additional details. The fourth century Gospel of Nicodemus holds a place of special importance in the development of the traditions. It relates how Joseph, having been imprisoned in a windowless room for his central role in the burial of Christ, is miraculously released at the very moment of the Resurrection. Some versions have Joseph later being bricked into a massive wall for teaching the Gospel. He is discovered years after, alive and unharmed, having been sustained by light and food from heaven.[30]

These and other traditions[31] garnered from this apocryphal gospel and its variants, form the basis for much of Robert de Boron's *Roman de l'Estoire dou Graal*. Probably composed at the end of the twelfth century, this great synthesis of esoteric traditions focuses on the relation of Joseph of Arimathea to the Holy Grail—the latter being a symbol of the Center par excellence. It tells how Joseph uses the cup of the Last Supper to catch the blood that flowed from Christ's wounds at the Crucifixion. He hides the cup and is later imprisoned. There Christ appears to him and gives him the same cup to sustain him for the time he will remain in prison. When Joseph asks what he has done to deserve such a gift, Christ responds "Thou didst take me down from the Cross and lay me in thy sepulchre. . . ."[32] Joseph becomes the Grail bearer precisely because he is intimately connected to the cosmic mysteries of the Cross and the Tomb.

According to other legends Joseph of Arimathea traveled to Glastonbury, England, bearing with him the vessel of the Grail. It is said that when he arrived he stuck his staff into the top of a hill and lay down to rest. When he awoke, the staff had rooted. It grew into a tree that burst into flower every year on Christmas Day. In our chapter on the Axis we saw how the staff of the wood of the Paradisal Tree flowered for another Joseph—the carpenter. We noted then that the staff was a symbol of the World Axis. A similar interpretation applies here, emphasized in the threefold configuration of staff, tree, and hill or mountain. Moreover, the very fact that the bearer of the staff and the Grail had a leading role in the events surrounding the Crucifixion reminds us of the close links among Axis, Cross, Center, and Holy Sepulcher.

At one point in de Boron's *Graal*, Jesus tells Joseph that in the future "tables" (or altars) will be set up, then says:

> The table signifies the Cross; the vessels in which the sacrifice and consecration will be made signify the grave wherein thou didst lay me. This is the cup in which my body will be consecrated in the form of the Host. The paten that will be laid upon

it signifies the stone with which thou didst close the mouth of the tomb, the cloth that will be spread over it signifies the linen that thou woundest round my body.[33, 34]

This symbolism is linked to what de Boron calls "the Great Sacrament of the Grail," really a kind of cosmic Mass. The energies involved in the events of the Crucifixion, Descent to the UnderRealm, and Resurrection are invoked each time the ceremony is performed. The created order symbolized by the Cross and the table or altar is the stage for this spiritual activity.

We are dealing with a truing, or redemption, of the cosmos. The theme is elaborated upon in de Boron's later description of the table set up by Joseph and of the ceremony performed there: When the land becomes barren, Joseph prays for help before the vessel of the Holy Grail. He is instructed to set up a table and to place the Grail vessel at its center. Of those who come to participate in the ceremony only the pure in heart are able to approach the table and receive the grace of the Grail. The land is restored when those who cannot perceive the power of the Grail leave the community. In other words, the regeneration of the cosmos requires the mediation of those who have placed themselves in correct relation to the Center.

Allied to this theme we have again the doctrine of the interdependency of macrocosm and microcosm, a perception of the great chain of being linking the universe and its denizens. Because of their awareness of this inherent synergy between creator, cosmos, and man, ancient writers, artists, and builders attempted to replicate, in symbolic fashion, the image of a perfected universe—incorporating, wherever possible, cosmic correspondences into their work.

As far as Christian lore is concerned, such correspondences are particularly evident in the layout of sacred buildings. A striking example relevant to our current discussion is found in a passage from Procopius of Gaza (ca. 540). He describes the plan of a church in Constantinople:

The lines were drawn in the form of a cross, joining one another in the middle, the upright one pointing to the rising and the setting sun, and the other cross line towards the north and south wind. These were surrounded by a circuit of walls, and within by columns placed both above and below; at the crossing of the two straight lines, that is, about the middle point of them, there is a place set apart that may not be entered except by the priests, and which is consequently termed the sanctuary.[35]

Here the whole building is aligned with natural forces—the course of the sun and the winds. Furthermore, since this church (like most sacred edifices) incorporates the symbolism of the cross, it mirrors the spiritual structure of the universe. On one level, we have an image of the mystical body of Christ laid upon the Cosmic Cross. On another level, we have a likeness of the human body. Durandus of Mende (ca. 1100) states explicitly, "The form of the church corresponds to the parts of the human body."[36]

Peter of Celle (1187) calls the nave of a church a "belly" or "womb" (*venter*), and the chevet he calls the "head" (*caput*).[37]

Maximus the Confessor (580–662), remarks that the church is a figure of God, an image of the world "composed of visible and invisible substances," and a likeness of the human being—body, soul, and spirit.[38] Included in the symbolism of the church (or at least certain churches) is the entire complex of subtle psychic and spiritual energies that underpin physical human existence.

In short, the church is a reflection of the total human being, just as it is a mirror of the whole of the cosmos. At the center of all is the Sacred Heart. Represented in the church by the sanctuary and the altar, it is at once the heart of God, the Cosmic Center, and the heart or center of the human being.

In addition to being the esoteric basis for the design of ancient churches, the three-dimensional Cosmic Cross flowing forth from the sacred center provides the essential model for the theurgic rites of mediation. This is an important point. Most modern Christian adepts generally have little opportunity to openly exercise their gifts and traditions within an actual physical church of the right layout and proportion. Although some known to us have special house-based chapels (as in the early days of Christianity), most improvise space as best they can, relying upon an inner or ritual model of the Cross to link to the

Center—to the point where "the power of God, flowing together from the four quarters, stands still."

The exercise below (and the one that follows the next chapter) is based in part upon just such a model.

The Sun Chalice

*S*tart with the kenosis meditation, then recite the phrase for the Sphere of Creation, becoming aware of a sphere of light building around you, its boundaries coinciding with the boundaries of your aura.

The sphere expands. As it grows, its light separates into innumerable points that flash as stars upon a backdrop of indigo darkness.

Recite the phrase for the Lance of Light and become aware of the axis of light running through the poles of the cosmic sphere and through the line of your spinal column.

Now chant the phrase for the Living Flame. You are conscious of a stream of golden fire descending along the line of the axis. It passes though your spinal column and descends to the center of the earth, kindling there a secret fire. The stream of fire rises, entering the base of your spine, and rushes up to your head before it fades into a single golden flame in your heart.

Look into the center of the flame. Its golden radiance grows, becoming so bright that you feel as if the sun itself were rising within you.

Out of this brightness, you perceive patches of color. These sharpen into a landscape, similar to the landscape of your pre-

vious visions, but now transfigured into a likeness of the earthly paradise.

You stand upon the world mountain. Immediately before you rises a great cosmic tree, its heaven-spread branches filled with flaming leaves and luminous fruit.

These, you realize, correspond with the cosmic planes and levels of being. You are aware also, in translucent vision, of the roots of the tree spreading throughout the mountain, deep into the earth, touching upon a series of wondrous crystal caves. Here lie the mighty elemental forces that shape the world, and you acknowledge them with a ritual gesture of respect.

Near the base of the tree you see a huge glowing emerald, its surface carved with arcane symbols. From a cleft in this sacred stone springs the source of the four world rivers.

You look at the magical landscape around you and marvel at the redolent verdure and life which emanates from every detail. You are aware of many animals in the landscape, not only the more familiar birds and beasts of the world but also mythical creatures such as the unicorn and the phoenix. You are conscious also of a great host of elemental and angelic beings, including the guardians of this hidden realm, by whose leave you have entered here, and whose very presence seems to sound a chorus to the ineffable beauty of this secret place.

And you become aware of the companionship of inner plane adepts, among them mysterious presences of deep spiritual authority—masters, saints, and magi—who instill within you a profound sense of peace.

You are drawn to gaze again upon the emerald stone.

As you do so you are aware of a shift in your consciousness and you feel a strengthening within you of the link between the realm of imaginal symbols and the world of pure spirit.

You see a great mandorla appear above the stone, its outline faint at first, but quickly growing into an almond of golden light. As you look into this light, you see, translucently silhouetted within it, a mighty figure of the cosmic Christ, royal, crowned and robed, his palms pressed together before his heart in the familiar position of prayer.

He looks down upon the assembled company, then stretches out his arms in a gesture of blessing. As his hands part before him, a six-pointed cross of light bursts forth from his heart, raying out to the height and depth and length and breadth of the cosmos, offering a blessing of love, power, and wisdom to the entire created order in all its visible and invisible aspects.

And now there comes from within the central point of the cross a rush of radiance. You are enveloped by an immeasurable illumination. You realize that in some mysterious way your being has been touched by the Source of all being.

The light fades, and with it fades the paradisal vision, leaving you once again conscious of yourself at the center of the star-covered cosmic sphere. The sphere contracts, drawing the stars together into one sphere of pure starlight. You are aware also of the lance of light running through your spinal column and through the poles of the aura-sized sphere that now encompasses you.

And deep within your heart is the spark of golden fire. Out of the root of this flame, fine lines of bright, golden-white light, like the rays of the sun, shoot up, weaving themselves into the form of a cup, a veritable sun chalice.

You meditate upon the meaning of this symbol at the center of your being, reciting, as you do so, the selected ritual phrase (suggestions: "a chalice in the sacred heart," "blessed are those who seek the grail," or "be hallowed by a holy grail.").

CHAPTER FIVE

The WHEEL of LIFE

he Wheel of Life is a practical esoteric key based on a primordial fourfold or sevenfold (or both) division of time and space. It is based, that is, on the fourfold seasonal cycle of spring, summer, fall, and winter; the cycle of the day as expressed in the points of dawn, midday, dusk, and midnight; the lunar cycle; the rotational rising and setting of the stars; and the four cardinal directions of east, south, west, and north. In sevenfold form these cycles and divisions combine with linear or axial models of time and space: past, present, future and below, center, above.

However configured, the patterns of sacred time and space always have biological, psychic, and spiritual harmonics within creation. Indeed, according to esoteric teaching the patterns of creation are themselves "mirrors" of divinity. And it is no surprise that we find in the early strata of Christian lore and tradition a fair number of references to this reflective or symbolic property of the cosmos. In the third century, for instance, Cyprian of Carthage wrote:

> It is in imitation of the Lord himself that the sun completes the
> 365 days of the year and the fourfold division of the day. Now

71

each of these four divisions of the day has three hours in it. And three of the hours carry the image of those three days that in the beginning of time were without sun or moon. Likewise those three (primordial) days were revealed in the adding of three hours four times over four years to produce one (extra) day of twelve hours; and in the four seasons of three months each; and in the twelve month course of the year. Thus, through multi-form threefoldness, the twelve hours have been displayed in the four divisions of the one Gospel. And the three months in the course of (each of) the four seasons, that is in the course of the four Gospels, have revealed to us the Twelve Apostles chosen by Christ.[1]

In this passage, Cyprian presents the essentials of a model of sacred time. He begins by designating the annual and diurnal cycles of the Sun as *imitationes Christi*. He then develops the idea, correlating the primordial creation with the cycle of the day. In accordance with the ancient sundial, a cycle of twelve hours is given, with one quarter of these in darkness. These three hours of darkness (equivalent to six hours in modern time) resonate with the three days of darkness before the creation of the sun and moon at the beginning of time (see Gen. 1).

The same primordial processes are repeated or reflected in the year of four seasons and twelve months. Fused with this temporal structure are the symbolic patterns of the twelve Apostles and the four Gospels, which have analogies in the twelve hours of the fourfold day and the twelve months of the fourfold year.

Just as Cyprian's work places the four Gospels in relation to sacred time, so do other authors relate these holy stories to the shape of sacred space. The second century bishop Irenaeus,[2] for example, remarks upon their accordance with the structure of the cosmos as follows:

The Gospels could not be either greater or lesser in number than they are. For since there are four regions of the world in which we live, and four Universal Spirits, and since the Church is disseminated over the whole earth, and the pillar and firmament of the Church is the Gospel and the Spirit of Life; it follows that she should have four pillars breathing forth incorruptibility in all directions and vivifying people everywhere.[3]

For Irenaeus, there are four Gospels precisely because there are four regions or quarters to the world. Irenaeus goes on to comment upon the four kerubic creatures[4] ascribed to the four evangelists and Gospels: lion, ox, eagle, man. On the one hand, he remarks, the animals and Gospels symbolize four "dispensations" of Christ through the ages as logos, praxis ("a priestly and liturgical practice"), cosmic spirit (literally "the Celestial Spirit over all the Earth"), and man. On the other hand the kerubic images correspond with four ages or epochs: the Adamic Age, the Age of Noah, the Age of Moses, and the Fourth Age (of the Christos or, perhaps, of Mary) which "renovates man and recapitulates all within itself through the (fourfold) Gospel."

Of particular interest also is Irenaeus's mention of the four Universal Spirits associated with the four quarters. These are likely the four archangels Raphael, Michael, Gabriel, and Uriel. Although the first three names are still familiar to many people, the name of the fourth archangel, Uriel (or Auriel), is not well known. In point of fact, however, the four were closely allied in ancient times. The four archangels are mentioned individually in certain books of the Bible and Apocrypha.[5] They appear together in the esoteric *Epistle of the Apostles* (second century), where they are said to have accompanied Christ into the fifth sphere of the heavens. Isidore of Seville (560–636) also mentions the four by name and outlines their attributes. The fact that the political church banned the veneration of Uriel at the Council of Rome in 745 also suggests the archangel played a role of some significance in the folk-magical traditions of Europe.

The archangels may be seen as four great guardian beings, as stewards or caretakers of creation with special relationships to cosmic cycles and structures (figure 8). They are generally assigned to the four directions as follows: Raphael in the east, Michael in the south, Gabriel in the west, and Uriel in the north. The names of the archangels also suggest aspects of their spiritual role in creation: Raphael, "healer of God," has much to do with healing and guiding energies. Michael, "likeness of God," is on one level concerned with enabling the interchange of spiritual power between the Realms, and on another with high mystical experiences of an apocalyptic type where consciousness of all worlds and planes passes away as the soul joins in direct union with Ultimate Being. Gabriel, "power or strength of God," has to do with creative and purifying energies. Uriel, "light or radiance of God," has to do with the mediation of the inner light of wisdom to the outer world.

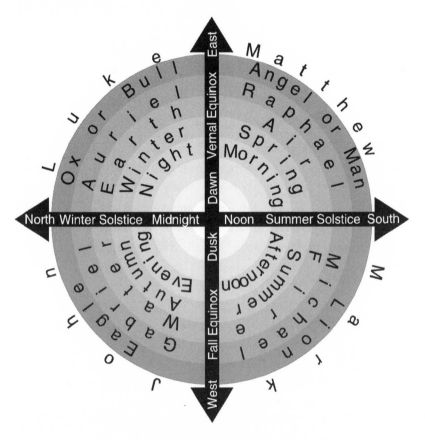

Figure 8. *The Wheel of Life: The relation of the archangels to cosmic cycles and structures*

We might add to our quaternal model of cosmic energies the attributes of the four elements. Methodius of Olympus (ca. 312), for example, links the elements to the kerubic creatures as follows: The

man or angel corresponds to air, the ox to earth, the lion to fire, and
the eagle to water. "God, then, . . . holding air and earth, water and
fire in his hand and ruling them by his will, like a four-horsed char-
iot, in an unutterable way controls the universe and keeps it in
being."[6] The four elements characterize the "psychic substance" of
the universe. They express certain energies or principles of creation—principles that are naturally reflected in the soul and life of
humankind. Very briefly: Air is the element of activity, light, clarity,
abstraction, impulse and repulse and corresponds to the mental nature.
Fire symbolizes growth, life, illumination, consummation, transformation, the desire nature. Water cleanses, forms, purifies, fills and
empties; it is depth and love, the emotional nature. Earth is concerned
with the energies of solidity, patterning, steadfastness, law, shaping
and transforming through pressure, the physical nature.

Where this concern with fourfold symbolism is leading is to the
recognition or recovery of a great system of correspondences based
upon the mystery of the Cosmic Cross. As we saw in the last chapter
the Cosmic Cross represents the underlying unified spiritual structure
of the universe—a structure ultimately identified with the mystical
body of Christ. A Coptic apocryphal gospel tells how at the birth of
Christ a star appears in the form of a wheel, its figure like a cross—in
other words a circled cross. On the cross are emblazoned the words
"this is Jesus the Son of God." This image of star-wheel or circled cross
expresses at least two levels of significance. On one hand, the image
fulfills a conventional function as a sign pointing to the place where
the Christ Child is born. On the other hand, the image is itself a
symbol of the Christ nature. In the latter case, the words "this is
Jesus the Son of God" refer to the mysteries of the cosmic Christ as
expressed through the universal symbolism of the circled cross.
Irenaeus also writes on the theme of the cosmic Christ:

> Now seeing that he is the Logos of God Almighty, who in
> unseen wise in our midst is universally extended in all the
> world, and encompasses its length and breadth and height and
> depth—for by the Logos of God the whole universe is ordered
> and disposed — in it is crucified the Son of God, inscribed

crosswise upon it all: for it is right that he, being made visible, should set upon all things visible the sharing of his Cross, that he might show his operation on visible things through a visible form. For he it is who illuminates the height that is the heavens; and encompasses the deep that is beneath the earth; and stretches and spreads out the length from east to west; and steers across the breadth of north and south; summoning all that are scattered in every quarter to the knowledge of the Father.[7]

Once again the Bishop of Lyon is concerned primarily with sacred space. Here, however, the horizontal plane of the four directions has developed a central vertical axis—the cosmic circled cross expressed in three dimensions. We have met with this figure of the three-dimensional cross before, in particular, in a passage from the *Clementine Homilies*, where it was shown to be the primordial pattern underlying the manifestation of sacred event, space, and time. Sacred space has not only a horizontal polarity of length and breadth expressed as regions, quarters, directions, but also a vertical polarity of Celestial Realm and UnderRealm—all arrayed round a central primordial point. Time may also be said to have a horizontal plane manifested through the cosmic cycles of sun, moon, and stars (as in the seasons, day, months, and zodiac) and a linear or vertical axis running from the past, through the eternal present, and into the future. Properly speaking, we are dealing with a flow of energies that are neither cyclic nor linear, but spiral. The pattern forms the basis for the structure and action of ritual; the design of the church, temple, or ritual area; and, of course, the ritual calendar.

As symbolic glyphs built upon the general pattern of the Wheel of Life, all sacred calendars are primordial, perennial, and universal. In terms of their precise details, however, considerable fluidity is involved. In the following discussion we have not deemed it necessary to adhere to any rigid designation of dates. We have, however, tried to strike a balance between tradition, esoteric teaching, and intuitive perception. Our concerns are not with the nostalgic commemoration or celebration of "historical" events or activities per se. We are here primarily interested in the magical and initiatory aspects of the sacred calendar.

The sacred calendar of Magical Christianity has two main components. The more important of the two we term the Christological cycle, and the other the sanctoral cycle. The former deals with the magical life of Christ, the latter with the esoteric significance of the legendary acts of the apostles, saints, and angels.

Looking at the overall pattern of the Christological cycle we note that all the main events take place roughly within one half of the year, with a high concentration near the winter solstice and the spring equinox (figure 9). This placment near the focal points of solstice and equinox gives a cosmic emphasis to the experiences of resurrection, rebirth, and regeneration that lie at the heart of the tradition of Magical Christianity. For both these points have to do with the seasonal increase of light and cosmic energy in the world. The winter solstice

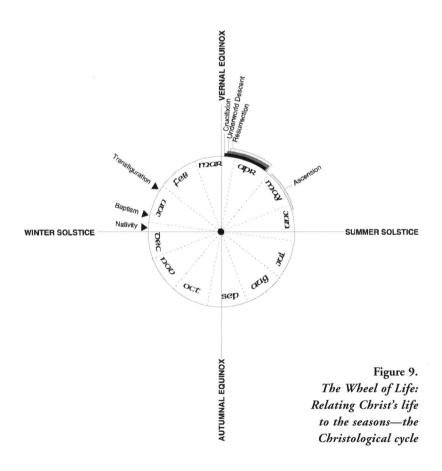

Figure 9.
The Wheel of Life:
Relating Christ's life
to the seasons—the
Christological cycle

marks the juncture in the year when the days begin to progressively lengthen. The spring equinox heralds the beginning of days that are longer than the nights (figure 10).

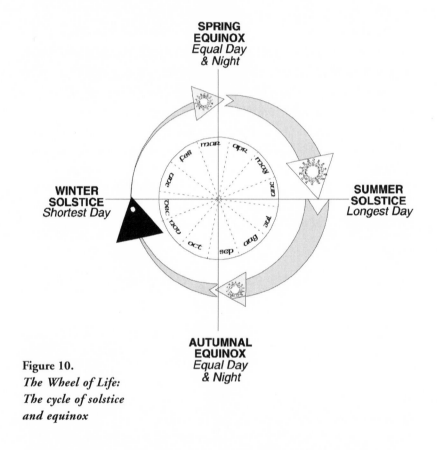

Figure 10.
The Wheel of Life:
The cycle of solstice
and equinox

Great psychic tides are associated with the solstices and equinoxes. In fact, the entire year is encompassed by an overlapping ebb and flow of cosmic energies. These surges of energy can be tapped through ritual and meditation and are a great store of inner power for adepts of all esoteric traditions.

The energies released at the solstices and equinoxes are mirrored in the rotational pattern of the four seasons. These in turn resonate with the fourfold cycle of the day and with the lunar cycle. The round of the cosmic tides also finds its reflection in the human life cycle and in the patterns of human activity. For all has its rise, apogee, decline, and fall.

It might be useful to briefly tabulate some of the processes involved in the fourfold cosmic cycle. Meditation upon the following list of keywords will deepen one's understanding of these cyclic energies:

solstice	equinox	solstice	equinox
winter	spring	summer	autumn
storing	sowing	tending	harvesting
gestating	germinating	flowering	wilting
inbreathing	inbreathing	outbreathing	outbreathing
midnight	dawn	noon	dusk
night	morning	afternoon	evening
nadir	ascent	apogee	descent
set	arising	risen	descending
originating	developing	establishing	completing
birth	youth	maturity	death
afterlife	birth	life	death
new	waxing	full	waning
empty	filling	full	emptying
low	flow	high	ebb

The Christological component of the esoteric calendar has to do, as we have said, with the magical life of Christ. In this, there are seven key initiations or mysteries. These have much to do with the ongoing release of regenerative spiritual energies throughout the Three Cosmic Regions and the Planes of Being.

The archetypal pattern of the Christ's life provides an exemplary model for certain types of inner experience and mediatory or theurgic practice. There is space here to deal only with the major images, and those only in brief, but this outline should more than suffice to show the importance of the pattern as a whole:

1. The Nativity (December 25). At one time, the Nativity was celebrated as part of Epiphany, on January 6 or 7. It was moved, in the fourth century, to the twenty-fifth of December to have it coincide with the Roman feast of *Sol Invictus*, a celebration of the birth of the Unconquered Sun. Originally the Nativity may have been a movable feast like Easter, because we are obviously concerned with the winter solstice, which occurs between the twenty-first and twenty-third of December each year. The winter solstice is the point at which the days, having reached their shortest duration, now begin to lengthen. Symbolically light wins out over darkness. More than this, however, we must consider that at the solstice, the energies of the earth are most indrawn. Plant and animal life is contained within the earth to its fullest extent. The angelic and elemental powers connected with vegetation and growth are also withdrawn into the earth. It is at this moment, the moment when the earth is most fecund, most pregnant with cosmic energy, that the divine child is born in the depths of a cave.

The Christ Child is closely tied to the very structure of nature. One might say the divine child manifests at the center of nature. According to one legend, at the birth of the Christ Child "the sun in the east bowed down, the stars stood still, the mountains and the forests shook and touched the earth with their summits and the heaven and earth were bowed."

Further, we know from the legends and from the timing of Christmas and Epiphany[8] that the divine child is intimately linked with the cycles of the sun and moon. These two represent polarity, male and female, active and receptive, and so on.

In fact, contained within the polar symbolism of the sun and moon as linked to the Christ Child we have a definite remnant of at least a part of the original intent of Christianity. Namely, it was to present a balanced alternative to the severely patriarchal religion of the Old Testament. There was originally an attempt to balance the male and female energies of the soul. Had it not been for certain so-called "Pauline" influences within the political church, more elements of this balance might well have been retained. Nonetheless, it is interesting to note here that as a symbol the divine child is an androgynous being, balancing male and female, unifying the sun and the moon.

We are beginning to get a picture of the function and significance of the birth of the Christ Child as an archetypal event. We might summarize this picture as follows:

- The Christ Child unifies opposites.
- The Christ Child represents the Center, both of our own personal being and, by extension, of the collective being, of nature, and of the planetary being. Another way of putting this is to say that the Christ Child is the spiritual center of the cosmos.

It should be reasonably apparent that the symbolic significance of the divine child meshes with the meaning and inner structure of the Christmas period to form a coherent whole, all of which must be taken into account when we speak of the inner meaning of the Nativity.

2. The Baptism (January 6). As a cosmic event the Baptism of Christ involves the drawing together, fusion, and release into the Terrestrial Realm of Celestial and UnderRealm forces. The latter are symbolized by the elements of fire and water, respectively—fire representing the power of the spirit and water the principle of primordial potency. Referring to Christ's Baptism, Clement of Alexandria writes, "The new creation comes about by water and the spirit, like the creation of the universe: The spirit of God was borne upon the waters."[9]

According to art and legend, when Jesus descended into the Jordan it was enflamed, and when he rose from it the water also rose seething around him. There is an ancient tradition cited by Cyril of Jerusalem in the fourth century that the river Jordan issued forth from the mouth of a dragon. The river is thus the dragon's breath, the cosmic *kundalini*, which is lifted up and consecrated by the Christ being. At the same time, according to some traditions, the spirit descends from above in the form of a fiery dove.

The resulting fusion of the energies of above and below and their dispersal or mediation into the Terrestrial Realm transforms the world by drawing it into closer configuration with its prototype. As Gregory of Nyssa writes in his *De baptismo*, after Christ's Baptism the Jordan enveloped the entire world, and following along the channels of the four rivers that flow out from the earthly paradise "carried back into paradise things far more precious than those which came out."[10] This is the irradiation of the world by the great cosmic dragon force. Now "christified" or consecrated, it transfigures the entire world by transforming its paradisal protoype. Through the mystery of the Baptism the earthly paradise is reconfigured to the pattern of a new creation.

3. The Transfiguration (January 20). The Transfiguration complements the mystery of the Nativity. For while the Nativity occurs in the context of UnderEarth symbolism (Christ is born amidst the creational energies in the depths of the womb of the earth mother, also in darkness, in a cave, and so on), the Transfiguration takes place on a mountain, that is, within the context of the Celestial or OverRealm powers. The mountain where Christ's Transfiguration occurred is traditionally said to have been Mount Tabor, a name that derives from *tabbur*, meaning "navel." In other words, the Tranfiguration occurs at the Center, on the World Mountain. In sacred lore, the ascent of the World Mountain is always an ascent through the heavens and Planes of Being. At the peak is the dark cloud—a symbol of the unfathomable divinity of nonbeing, or uncreated reality.

On a cosmic level, the mystery of the Transfiguration involves a rupture or breach of the Planes bringing the divine reality into direct contact with the physical and psychic Planes. This opening of a gateway between the worlds also enables contact with the higher orders of adepts, saints, and masters, which in the tradition of the Transfiguration are represented by the figures of Moses and Elijah. Moreover, Christ takes several of his initiates with him to the mountain, where to a degree they participate in the Transfiguration.

The Transfiguration thus provides a model for "deification," that is, for the enlightenment or illumination of the initiate.

As Saint Gregory Palamas writes, "The deifying gift of the Spirit is a mysterious light, and transforms into light those who receive its richness."[11] And elsewhere in the same work the author remarks how some of the saints "have seen this light as a limitless sea, flowing forth in a paradoxical manner from the unique Sun, that is, from the adorable Body of Christ, as in the case of the apostles on the Mountain. It is thus that the first fruits of our human constitution are deified."[12] Because of this connection to the body of Christ, the Transfiguration is also especially linked with the ritual pattern of Holy Communion.

4. The Crucifixion (three days prior to the Resurrection). We have mentioned several times in this book the significance of the three-dimensional cross as an extension or creational development of the Cosmic Center. This cross is the great symbol both of cosmic unity and of the realignment of the cosmic order. The world is redeemed because it is fused with the Divine Being who is, in the words of Irenaeus, "inscribed crosswise upon it all." Maximus the Confessor speaks of the crucified Christ as "he who encloses in himself all beings. . . . As the center of straight lines that radiate from him he does not allow by his unique, simple, and single cause and power that the principles of beings become disjoined at the periphery, but rather he circumscribes their extension in a circle [or sphere] and brings back to himself the distinctive elements of beings who he brought into existence."[13]

The Crucifixion of Christ on one level, then, is nothing less than his mergence with the universe and all who live and move and have their being therein. As the Gospel of Thomas lyrically expresses it:

> I am the light that is over all things.
> I am all:
> all came forth from me,
> and all attained to me.
> Split a piece of wood,
> and I am there.
> Pick up a stone,
> and you will find me there.[14]

It is the promise of this universal vision that places the Crucifixion as an initiatory image in certain magical Christian rituals. These rites involve opening the soul to an awareness of the immeasurable workings of divinity within the cosmos. During the experience the individual ego "dies" to itself and is reconfigured to the higher self. This is one reason initiation earns the epithet "living death." There is a realignment of the human soul, a redemption, resurrection, or reattunement to a primordial spiritual vision. The life energy of the initiate is no longer primarily focused on personal development or enlightenment, but turns now to matters of cosmic mediation.

5. The Descent to the UnderRealm (three days between Crucifixion and Resurrection). On a cosmic level, the Descent to the UnderRealm involves the emptying, restructuring, and realignment of the energies of the UnderEarth. According to ancient traditions,[15] through Christ's Descent, the UnderEarth is emptied, souls are freed, "the abysses are opened and closed," death is conquered. The Under-Realm is reconfigured according to the cosmic pattern of the cross (in the Gospel of Nicodemus, Christ sets up a cross of light in the UnderRealm). Moreover the primal man, Adam, is restored to paradise and the way to the Paradisal Tree, that is, to the powers of the Cosmic Axis, is reopened. These transformations in the UnderEarth structure make certain initiatory experiences available to the individual soul.

The way to "paradise" is eased: The unconscious or hidden reaches of the soul are emptied of their "infernal" or "demonic" elements, easing passage through the UnderRealm reaches. John Chrysostom says that into the darkness of the UnderRealm "the sun of Righteousness descended and lightened it, making Heaven of Hades."[16] In esoteric traditions, "paradise" is reached by traveling through the UnderRealm.

The Descent to the UnderRealm involves the reattunement of those UnderEarth forces that shape the world as we know it. In one sense, the UnderRealm is restored to its primal form—the fecund cosmic womb, the place of spiritual rebirth and recreation, the point of Resurrection.

6. The Resurrection (first full moon after spring equinox). In canto 23 of the *Paradiso*, Dante has a vision of the "shining substance" of the Risen Christ. The vision takes place in the eighth sphere of the heavens, that is, the region of the zodiac and the fixed stars. Dante's vision accords with early traditions that speak of Christ's Resurrection as occurring on the "eighth day." In ancient cosmology the seven days of the week correspond to the seven planetary spheres of the visible heavens. An "eighth day," according to this reckoning, would represent the eighth celestial sphere, that is, the *ogdoad* or sphere of the fixed stars.

This symbolism of the mystery of the Resurrection suggests at once both the incarnation within the earthly sphere of the primordial, perfect, "zodiacal man" and the raising up of the physical plane itself to the level of the archetypes. In one sense, Christ's resurrection body is of an archetypal "stellar" or "sidereal" nature, with the power to utterly regenerate the cosmos. In speaking of the reason why spring is the most appropriate time for the Resurrection, Eusebius remarks,

> This time was the very one which appeared at the moment of the first creation of the world, when the earth brought forth shoots and the stars appeared; it is at this time that the Lord of the whole world celebrated the mystery of his own feast and, like a great star, appeared to light up the whole world . . . and thus to bring back the anniversary of the cosmos.[17]

Another reason the Resurrection is linked closely to springtime is that the vernal equinox marks the moment from which daylight begins to outlast night. Light becomes the predominant force in the world, and hence it is now that the teachings of light are given out to the Apostles. The period following the Resurrection constitutes a higher octave of the time following the Baptism, when Jesus first began his mission as teacher and healer. This is why nearly all of the esoteric apocryphal works claim to present a hidden teaching or gnosis received directly from the Risen Christ (e.g., Gospel of Thomas, Acts of John, Acts of Peter, and apocryphal Gospel of John), as in this hymn quoted by Hippolytus:

> Let me disclose all secrets;
> Let me reveal the forms of all gods;
> And the hidden mystery of the Way
> Called Gnosis, let me impart.[18]

7. The Ascension (forty days after the Resurrection). Certain of the teachings ascribed to the Risen Christ concern knowledge of the spiritual structure of the cosmos (i.e., the nature of the various Planes and heavens), the mysteries of Christ's descent and ascent through the cosmic spheres, and instruction regarding the passage of the soul through the celestial spheres.

On one level, Christ's Ascension completes a cosmic "circuit" of spiritual force. Early legends, for instance, mention Christ descending through the seven spheres at the Incarnation. As he descends, he takes on a different form according to the nature of each sphere and thus remains unrecognized by its denizens.

The work of the Incarnation takes place incognito, the transformation of the cosmos being wrought from within. Then in completion of the mission, Christ reascends through the Planes—this time openly and in full glory. The work of the Ascension thus completes the pattern of the christification of the cosmos.

The Three Cosmic Regions are infused with the Christ force. The Logos has become the nucleus of the whole created order. But the Ascension does not "end" at the highest heaven. For while the Divine Being permeates and encompasses all creation, it simultaneously transcends it. One might speak then of the Ascension giving way to a "Transcension"—Divine Being transcending itself in the unfathomable mystery of nonbeing. The pattern of the Ascension also underlies a specific *disciplinam arcani*. As "the Way," the Christ embodies the cosmic Planes. This is why in some traditions he is depicted as being of titanic proportions, "so large that his head reached to Heaven." [19] Participation in the mystical body of Christ (e.g., through the Eucharist) includes then the possibility of an experience of "rising on the planes," of passing to and fro among the realms of being, consciousness, and creation.

* * * * * *

The Ascent of Christ through the spheres finds a symbolic counterpoint in the descent of divine fire at Pentecost. Pentecost traditionally takes place fifty days after the Resurrection, which brings it generally within the influence of the tidal energies of the summer solstice. In one sense, it can be considered as a bridge between the mysteries of the Christological cycle and the sanctoral cycle. We touched upon the archetypal nature of the pentecostal experience in chapter 3. The ability of the Apostles to speak every language marks them as representatives of all humanity. It is at this time also that the Apostles are designated different regions of the world in which to heal and teach (Acts 2). It is well known that long before apostolic times the various regions of the known world were associated with the signs of the zodiac. Like the lands they visited the Apostles too were linked to the twelve zodiacal signs. We have already cited traditions that correlate the Apostles with the zodiac through their association with the twelve months of the year and the ancient system of the twelve-hour day.

Of additional interest is the tradition of Jesus's round dance. Found in the Acts of John, this is a ritual dance that takes place after the Last Supper. The twelve Apostles move in a circle around the Christ, the Lord of the Dance, who sings a cosmic hymn. The hymn itself has to do with the resolution of opposites and with a ritual lifting up of the soul, enabling it to view from a cosmic perspective the rounds of birth, life, death, and rebirth, of being and nonbeing. In the middle of the hymn are the following lines:

> The One Ogdoad sings praise with us. Amen
> The Twelve dance on high. Amen.
> The Whole on high joins in our dancing. Amen.
> Who dances not knows not what comes to pass. Amen.[20]

Note the reference to the sphere of the stars, the *ogdoad*. The "Twelve" who dance on high are both the twelve signs of the zodiac and the Apostles themselves, who are raised in vision to the plane of celestial archetypes. They become participants in the great dance of the cosmos. This attunement of one's being to the Wheel of Life, to the rhythms and measures of the cosmic dance, can awaken a kind of "prophetic" wisdom within the soul. One suddenly becomes aware of the great concourse and meaning of creation.

The sidereal or zodiacal aspect of the Apostles is also seen in the depictions of the table of the Last Supper as a round table. The round "agape table" is a standard feature in many of the fourth-century catacomb chapels of Malta. And in the *Queste du Saint Graal*, the Round Table set up by Merlin for the Grail knights signifies the roundness of the cosmos and the configurations of the planets, elements and stars.

St. Peter
called "the Rock" & "Keeper of the Keys."
Key apocryphal works:
Acts of Peter; Apocalypse of Peter

St. Matthias
called "the New Apostle."
Key apocryphal works:
Acts of Andrew & Matthias

St. Jude
called "the Shepherd"
& "Great-hearted One."
Key apocryphal work:
Apostolic History of Abdias

St. Simon
called "the Zealot."
Key apocryphal work:
Apostolic History of Abdias

St. James the Younger
called "the Just" & "Brother of the Lord."
Key apocryphal work:
Protevangelion

St. Matthew
called "the Publican."
Key apocryphal works:
Gospel of Matthew; Acts of Matthew

Figure 11.
An apostolic calendar

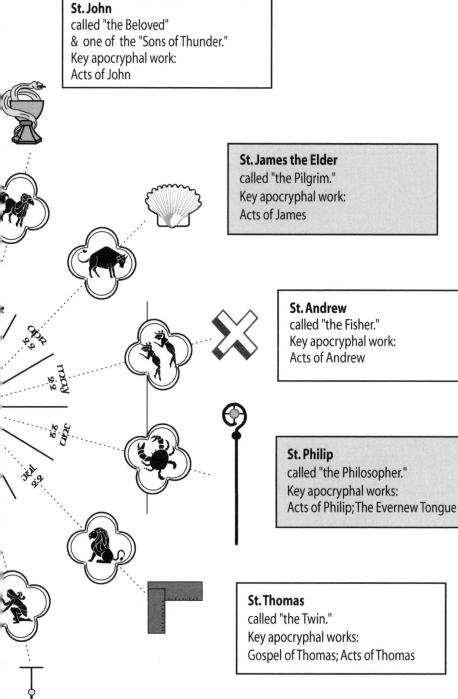

St. John
called "the Beloved"
& one of the "Sons of Thunder."
Key apocryphal work:
Acts of John

St. James the Elder
called "the Pilgrim."
Key apocryphal work:
Acts of James

St. Andrew
called "the Fisher."
Key apocryphal work:
Acts of Andrew

St. Philip
called "the Philosopher."
Key apocryphal works:
Acts of Philip; The Evernew Tongue

St. Thomas
called "the Twin."
Key apocryphal works:
Gospel of Thomas; Acts of Thomas

St. Bartholomew
called "the Husbandman."
Key apocryphal works:
Questions of Bartholomew;
Book of the Resurrection of Christ

The evidence connecting the Apostles to the zodiac points to a secret "calendar of saints" in existence since the earliest days of Christianity. More detailed explications of the esoteric significance of the Apostles will be taken up in forthcoming works.

For basic meditation and ritual purposes, however, we present here a simple chart of correspondences (figure 11). The innermost circle of the chart consists of the dates of the feasts of the twelve Apostles. These were determined by taking the ancient Feast of the Birth of Peter as a starting point and ascribing the Apostles to successive dates at one month intervals. Rather conveniently, the Feast of the Birth of Peter (February 22) corresponds to the entry of the sun into the zodiacal sign of Pisces.[21] The order of the Apostles is that found in Acts. Although the Four Gospels give variations on this order, Acts, as we have said, clearly suggests zodiacal correlations. These are shown in the second circle of the chart. Beyond this are some of the symbols associated with the Twelve. Beyond this again are the names and epithets of the Apostles, along with the titles of some of the more important and accessible apocryphal works associated with them.

It will be noted that a number of the apocryphal works we have cited are gospels, that is, they tell in some form of the acts, life, and words of Christ. There were, in early times, many more gospels than the four eventually canonized by the conventional church. Some of these apocryphal gospels have survived in their entirety; others are now partially or entirely lost. The four traditional Gospels have a special ritual importance in Magical Christianity, for, as we have seen, they are symbolically linked to the cosmic cycles of nature and man. In terms of content, they also reveal, in addition to many other esoterically significant elements, the basic initiatory pattern of the magical life of Christ. The apocryphal gospels fill out or supplement these mysteries. Taken collectively, the gospels, *all* gospels, constitute a great reservoir or repository of sacred lore and tradition.

There is, therefore, no notion in Magical Christianity of "scriptural authority" based upon a literal or "historical" reading of the Gospels. All sacred texts, including those of Christianity, are expressions of the many-faceted archetype of the Logos. Moreover, as symbolic manifestations of the Logoic essence, all sacred texts are also incomplete. They could not be otherwise, for they attempt to express a reality greater than themselves.

In conventional Christianity the term *Logos* is normally translated as "Word." But this convention is somewhat misleading, and even inaccurate. Logos is a numinous term that includes a whole range of meaning, depending on context. Among much else it denotes

- A tradition, treatise, or account—which might be written, oral, or in the form of symbolic images;
- The principle of order or configuration;
- The harmonizing principle of the cosmos;[22] and
- The creative principle of the cosmos.[23]

The latter three points, in particular, enable us to see why early writers such as Irenaeus identified the Logos with the Cosmic Cross (or alternatively with the crucified cosmic Christ) and hence with the patterns and rhythms of the Wheel of Life.

When we speak of the four Gospels as expressions of the Logos, we are speaking, on one level, of a theophany—a manifestation or revelation of divine reality—appearing through the structures and cycles of the cosmos. In this sense, "reading" the Gospels involves a spiritual participation in the rotation of the life force throughout the cycles of sacred time and within the shape of sacred space. We explore this further in the exercise that follows.

V I S I O N   E X E R C I S E   ～ CD Track 6
_____

The Secret Gospels

A fter the kenosis meditation, proceed as usual, reciting the appropriate phrases as you build up the symbols of the previous exercises: the Sphere of Creation, the Lance of Light, the Living Flame, and the Sun Chalice.

You find yourself in a great stone room or chapel, with each of the four walls dominated by a tall, massive, arched window filled with stained glass. In the darkened chamber you cannot clearly see the images contained within the glass.

Moving to the center of the room, you see four closed books resting on four stone lecterns, each facing one of the great windows. You approach the book before you, looking with awe at the finely tooled workmanship of its gold cover, richly inset with gems and jewels. You are moved to open the book. You see upon the page before you, drawn in wondrous illuminated letters, these words: **The people who sat in darkness have seen a great light.**

A gust of breeze touches your face and you look up to see the great window in front of you dissolve. You find yourself in the predawn twilight, gazing out toward the dark line of the horizon, which now begins to glow pale turquoise blue. Long shadows yield to increasing light as the solar orb begins to rise. A chorus of birdsong welcomes the springtide dawn. In the distance low bushes and tall trees display their new-life green. Nearby, budding flowers begin to sway in the gentle breeze, wafting their scents towards you.

Out of the light of the rising sun you see the figure of a winged man standing in the landscape. As his angelic face turns from contemplation of the dawning day towards you, you touch your hand to your heart, then raise it in salute to the mighty kerubic creature of the East.

And now over the entire scene, you are aware of the presence of the Archangel Raphael. A titanic figure of light, robed in swirls of sun-light gold and azure blue, the archangel holds a great and luminous crosier from the spiral of which come forth bursts of whirling wind. Amidst the spinning eddies of air is a host of luminous angelic and elemental beings. And you feel your spirit quickened by life-giving energy.

You close the golden book and see the window solidify, becoming a glorious scene of glass and light showing forth the figure of a winged man and beneath it, in ornate letters, the word **LIGHT**.

(pause for meditation)

Turning clockwise to your right you go now to the book in the South and looking upon its wonder, open it. There you see the illumined words: **To you has been given the secret of the Kingdom**.

The window fades and you become aware of the bright sun at noon. Its radiant light warms your skin and penetrates every pore of your body, energizing and regenerating you. You are aware of the flowers in full bloom, the trees and bushes bearing fruit and berry, the greenness of the grass and the richness of the land. Beneath the light of the daystar you become aware of the presence of a great lion who shakes his shaggy golden mane toward the summer sun, then lowers his head to look at you. And you salute the mighty kerubic creature of the South.

Over the entire scene is the towering presence of the Archangel Michael. See this great glorious being armored in red and golden light and bearing a great double-edged sword of fire and light. And you see a host of fiery angels and elementals streaming forth from the blazing light of the sword. You are momentarily bathed in an awareness of fiery warmth and transformative light.

You close the golden book. The stained glass solidifies, disclosing in radiant, jeweled light, the image of a golden lion and beneath it, in fiery letters, the word **LIFE**.

(pause for meditation)

You move again to your right, that is, to the West, and open the golden book. There you see, spelled out in illuminated letters, these words: **One sows and another reaps**.

The great window fades and you are aware of the quiet peace of an autumn evening. The trees are filled with leaves of red and orange and gold. The ground is covered with fruit and nuts and seed. In the distance, great fields of ripe grain sway in a gentle breeze. Immediately before you is a great river flowing strong and gracefully through the land. Looking out across the surface of the river you see, silhouetted against the orb of the setting sun, the figure of a mighty eagle, wings outspread in loving protection. Far-seeing eyes turn towards you as you salute the mighty kerubic creature of the West.

Overshadowing the entire scene is the Archangel Gabriel, a glowing figure of gigantic stature, swathed in flowing shades of deep blue and silver light, holding high a wondrous chalice of silver set with deep sapphire stones and intricately engraved with symbols. Above the rim of the chalice you see the crescent moon shining in the sky. Out of this mighty vessel, like a fount of sea foam, pours a great host of angelic and elemental beings in the colors of blue and sea green and of silver and foamy white. You feel yourself momentarily suffused with a rich, deep, encompassing love.

As you close the book, the glass of the western window solidifies, glowing deeply in shades of blue to display the figure of an eagle and beneath it, in ornate silver letters, the word **LOVE**.

(pause for meditation)

You move to the North and open the book, seeing there these words: **Behold, the Kingdom of God is within you.**

The window dissolves. You see a frosted landscape beneath the midnight winter sky. The trees and bushes are bare of leaves. The air is crystal clear. The night is moonless and the stars shine like a great sea of light across the heavens. You begin to pick out the constellations in their turning. You see them revolving like a great luminous wheel around the pole star.

Looking back at the landscape you see, standing at the crest of a hill, a mighty bull. Cold breath snorts from its nostrils as it paws the ground, releasing a rolling torrent of gems and crystals that gather in a heap of resplendent treasure at the foot of the hill. You see starlight reflecting in the multitude of shining stones. Then, the bull turns ageless eyes towards you in the utter clarity of impartial wisdom. And you salute the mighty kerubic creature of the North.

Over the entire scene, be aware of the presence of the Archangel Uriel, robed in dark indigo light with sparks of brilliant gold and silver flashing here and there. He holds a crystal paten, cunningly engraved with the secret patterns of the universe. From this paten rises, like a stream of shooting stars, a host of angelic and elemental beings.

You feel yourself momentarily filled with an intuitive awareness of the deepest cosmic mysteries.

You close the golden book and see the glass solidify into a dark, softly glowing mass of variegated green and brown light that shows the image of a bull and beneath it the word **LAW**.

(pause for meditation)

* * * * * *

The stone room fades from vision and you are aware of yourself once more at the center of the celestial sphere. The sphere contracts, bringing the stars together until they unite. And you find yourself enclosed in an aura-sized orb of pure starlight. You are aware, also, of the axis running through the poles of the orb, of the golden flame within your heart, and of the chalice woven out of the solar light of the flame.

Now, become aware of the sun chalice filling with light, which when it reaches the rim of the chalice, spills over in a great lightning flash that shoots out rays to the four directions: before and behind you, to your right and to your left; that is, to the East and to the West, to the South and to the North. As you meditate upon this great cosmic cross radiating from your heart, you intone an appropriate ritual phrase (suggestions: "a turning cross of life unfolding," "blessed are those upon the cross," or "be hallowed by a turning cross").

The CHRISTE REALMS

According to a very ancient and widespread tradition, the
Risen Christ gave out his secret name (or names) to the
Apostles. In esoteric practice, the name of Jesus constitutes a "key to the Kingdom of Heaven," a secret name of power giving access to the mysteries of the Three Realms, or Cosmic Regions,
and the Planes of Being: "God has highly exalted him and bestowed
upon him the name which is above every name, that at the name of
Jesus every knee should bow, in heaven and on earth and under the
earth" (Phil. 2:9–11).

We have made passing reference, throughout our previous chapters, to the idea of the Three Realms or Regions of the cosmos. These
are the Celestial Realm, the UnderRealm, and the Terrestrial Realm.
We shall here take a more detailed look at their structure and importance for esoteric work.

When speaking of the Terrestrial Region we are not referring
merely to the realm of physical phenomena. For from an esoteric point
of view—and this is the only one that concerns us here—the Terrestrial Realm includes what might be called an "etheric" dimension:
Expressions and currents of spiritual energies are sensed or envisioned

within the landscape. Certain features or constructs occurring or placed within the Terrestrial sphere give access to certain inner-world or spiritual energies.

The same distinctive elements provide nodal points of entry and exit for souls and psychic and spiritual energies flowing between the Regions and Planes.

Although visionary ascent to the Celestial heights or descent to the UnderRealm may take place from any power site or magical node, certain sites or features lend themselves through their intrinsic symbolism to certain types of inner-plane work and activity. Generally speaking, mountains, trees, hills, standing stones, towers, spires, pillars, mounds—indeed all those features that rise up, require climbing, ascending, or otherwise draw the soul upward—link with the Celestial Realm.

Indeed, in many cases the physical act of ascending is accompanied by a ritual or visionary rising on the Planes. Likewise, the features of descent include caves, grottos, springs, valleys, rivers, wells, tombs, crypts, catacombs, and so on. We also note that features such as caves, groves, temples, and other sacred enclosures typically contain symbolism that points to both the upper and lower Realms. And we have touched upon the universal significance of the tree as a symbol of the structure of all three Realms.

An interesting pattern of sacred caves and holy mountains occurs in the initiatory formula of the magical life of Christ:

Cave of Nativity	Mount of Transfiguration
Cave of Descent and Resurrection	Mount of Crucifixion
Cave of Ascension[1]	Mount of Ascension

Several of these features clearly express the tenor of the mysteries with which they are connected: the caves of the Nativity and of the Descent relate to the mysteries of the UnderRealm; the mounts of the Transfiguration and Ascension relate to the Celestial mysteries. The mount of the Crucifixion functions more as a nodal point, a symbolic center by which the entire creation, visible and invisible, is anchored, enabled and permeated with the Logoic presence.

The Cave of the Ascension serves to point up the close relationship between the Cosmic Axis and the Center. Central nodes are always found upon the Axis, just as the axial images always point to (or run through) the Center. Particular images merely serve to emphasize either the axial or nodal power in a given sacred site.

Taken together, the three sacred caves of Christian lore lead us deep into the mysteries of the divine feminine. Caves represent the dark womb of creation, the fecund center of pure potentiality whence all manifest form arises. Another facet of the archetype of the divine feminine is found in the traditions relating to the Holy Virgin Mother. In Magical Christianity, the Holy Mother appears in three main guises corresponding to the Three Realms. In her Terrestrial aspect, Mary appears in three roles: the mother of Jesus; the leader of the Apostles after the Resurrection, who brought to birth the Christian mysteries; and the redeemed Eve, that is, as an incarnation of the spirit of Life,[2] "the sleeping virgin now awakened."

The figure of Mary takes on even higher and deeper implications when contacted in her aspects of Star Maiden and Black Virgin. We give in table 1 a summary of the types of energies and polarities we are dealing with in these two figures:

Table 1. *The Polarities of*
Mary as Black Madonna and Star Maiden

Black Madonna	Star Maiden / Celestial Virgin
Mater Dolorosa	Queen of Heaven
Crystals, metals	Stars, planets
Elemental and angelic beings	Angelic and archangelic beings
Transmission of tradition through bloodlines	Spiritual transmission of tradition
Martyrs, champions, and hermits	Virgins, saints, and magi
The Taker	The Giver
The Unraveller	The Weaver
The way to the earthly paradise	The way to the New Jerusalem
UnderRealm	Celestial Realm

Obviously these correspondences offer a perspective rather different from the usual trivialized notions of "heaven and hell" doled out by the conventional church. In Magical Christianity, the Under-Realm descent complements the Celestial ascent. In its pure form, the UnderRealm journey corresponds with a "hard way" of initiation and may even result in instantaneous illumination. It is the way of the warrior or spiritual knight and requires in good measure the personal characteristics of strength, courage, initiative, action, skill, and self-sacrifice.

In the *Divine Comedy*,[3] Dante has a vision of the Church Militant in the earthly paradise and the Church Triumphant in the highest visible sphere of the heavens. These two facets of the Inner Church, for reasons we shall shortly discover, correspond to the UnderRealm and Celestial Realm journeys, respectively.

Underlying Dante's great initiatory poem, then, is the traditional model of Three Cosmic Realms or Regions. There are several ways of viewing this structure within the *Comedy*.

One way is to see the descent to the UnderRealm as a purely demonic experience, the Terrestrial experience as a purgatorial journey of suffering, and the Celestial journey as an extension of the purgatorial one, with ever-refined levels of purity and spiritual vision leading in the end to a divine vision and then a return to the earthly sphere.

A variant on this view—one that fits the intrinsic structure of the poem better—would see the Celestial mysteries in essentially the same manner: as a rising on the Planes until, at the highest levels, the vision fails or is swept aside by the unfathomable reality of Divine Being. The *Purgatorio*, however, and to some extent the *Paradiso* also, would be envisioned as an initiatory scenario that occurs simultaneously with, or even as an alternative to, the *Inferno*.

In other words, on one level the ascent of Mount Purgatory is also a descent to the UnderRealm, and simultaneously a rising through the Celestial spheres. We see this correspondence reflected in the integral structure of Dante's Regions (figure 12). The mount of purgatory occupies the same "space" as the pit of hell. The journey past the guardian at the center of the earth is, in a way, simultaneously a passage into the earthly paradise.

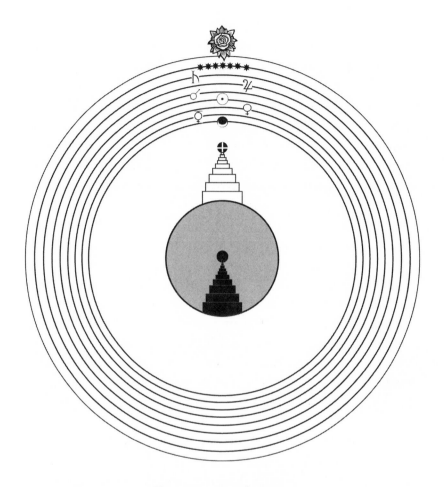

Figure 12. *Dante's cosmos*
The Mount of Purgatory, with the earthly paradise on its peak, is formed of the earth which was displaced by the fall of Lucifer, who lies head down at the center of the pit of Hell. Just as the Holy Mount is the higher aspect of the nether regions, so is the pattern of the Celestial Spheres a higher octave of the Mount of Purgatory.

In actual initiatory experience there is normally a certain crossing over or shifting between spheres of experience. Certain aspects of the experience will have to do with UnderEarth factors, others with Celestial contacts, and yet others with one's view of the Terrestrial Realm. Because so much depends upon the development of the individual soul, there is no telling beforehand exactly what this mix of energies will be or, for that matter, how the soul will react to them.

For any given individual the nature of this experience really depends upon factors such as spiritual integrity, personal destiny, courage, and a willingness to change for the better and to surrender the personal ego to a higher cause. To the degree the candidate is stubborn or flexible, egotistical or humble so will he or she experience alternatively the sufferings of hell,[4] the cleansing of purgatory, the wholeness of paradise, or the illumination of heaven. This is why mystery training is often so long and hard. To expose an unprepared soul to the powerful forces evoked during ritual initiation could indeed wreak havoc with that individual's personal life.

The idea that paradise or the "Edenic state" can be reached through a descent to the UnderRealm is not exclusive to Dante by any means. One sees the same process in the lives of certain of the very early saints, such as Macarius and Onuphrius, who journeyed perilously through the desert to live in caves or tombs, which were said to be located at the shortest possible distance from paradise. Also interesting are the medieval legends and tales that grew up around a cave on an island in Lough Derg, Ireland. Labeled Saint Brendan's Purgatory or more popularly Saint Patrick's Purgatory, the cave was widely known in medieval times and attracted pilgrims from all over Europe.

There was an abbey on the site and entry to the cave was gained, with permission of the abbot, through a special door located behind the high altar of the church. Tradition held that spending a night within this cave would absolve the pilgrim from the need to pass through purgatory after death. In other words it was a resolution of past (one is tempted to say karmic) "sins" or responsibilities, a living initiation here and now. It was common for the pilgrims to experience powerful visions during the ordeal. It is even said that some never returned from the cave, having vanished into the otherworld. One of the more famous pilgrims (one who did return!) was Owain Miles or Owain the Knight, whose tale is worth summarizing.

Owain was an English knight who had lived a life of dissipation and violence. In repentance he sought out the cave at Lough Derg that he might be purged of his sin and guilt. For fifteen days at the abbey he engaged in preliminary devotions and almsdeeds. Then he attended

Mass, was baptized, received the Sacrament, and followed the reliquary procession while the priests sang the litany. The door behind the altar was opened and he entered the darkness of the cave.

Sir Owain groped his way in the dark until he saw a glimmer of light. This grew brighter and brighter until he found himself in an inner land. Here there was a great hall and cloister peopled by men with shaven heads and white robes. They instructed Owain as to how to protect himself against evil spirits. Having received his instruction the Knight heard a great din and found himself in the midst of an onslaught of devilish beings. Using the teaching he had received for protection, however, he made his way further into the depths.

At one point he was pushed into a pit of molten metal by negative spirits, but escaped when he called upon the name of the Savior. He crossed a river of boiling pitch by means of a narrow, frail bridge, then came before a wall of glass, or crystal, in which was set a beautiful gate. Through this gate he came upon the land of paradise. This was so wondrous a place that the knight would have stayed if he could, but he was asked to return to the Terrestrial Realm.

And so return he did, but by a shorter, more pleasant path than that by which he had come. Owain was found at the door the next morning, waiting to be let out that he might recount his adventure. He afterwards went on a pilgrimage to the Holy Land and ended his days a man of renowned spirituality.[5]

The spiritual knight who would descend to the paradise needs preparation. In the story of Owain this takes the form of a special Mass, which ends with the knight being "sung" into the UnderRealm cave. There he meets inner helpers, Inner Plane adepts, who convey special knowledge or power to the candidate, without which he could not succeed or endure the ordeal.

Yet this knowledge requires the ability to set aside the ego, to surrender oneself to Divine Being, for it is this which ultimately "saves." There is likely an intended alchemical symbolism or resonance in the knight's ordeal of molten metal. Like the Great Work of the alchemist, the regeneration of the soul can only be finally attained with divine aid. It is no more possible to pull oneself through the UnderRealm by one's own power than it is to lift oneself into heaven by one's bootstraps.

Owain attains the paradisal realm and emerges a transformed being. The way back is easy and pleasant because the knight has succeeded in redeeming the unregenerate aspects of his soul.

All this ties in with traditional esoteric teaching regarding the Dweller on the Threshold. The Dweller on the Threshold is the guardian entity that blocks the initiate's passage through the portal of the mysteries. Such figures exist on several levels, but the common teaching is that the Dweller reflects the unredeemed elements of one's own soul. Normally one must acknowledge, accept, and learn to live with these elements, and by so accepting (far harder than it sounds), finds they are "redeemed." But this encounter rarely takes the form of frightening visions.

Instead it is generally experienced through events, relationships, emotions, desires, and so on that arise in the course of daily life. The UnderRealm journey involves, then, a coming to terms with the "lower" levels of (one's) being, a resolution of the drag of patterns of the past—usually from beyond the present life—and a reconnection with the Edenic state of existence. In very practical terms, this journey means clarifying and generally reconfiguring one's relationship to creation and to one's fellow creatures.

The obviously exemplary pattern for all this is Christ's Descent to the UnderRealm by means of which "death and hell" were conquered and the way opened to paradise. We have given an outline of the cosmic significance of this pattern in chapter 5.

The magical life of Christ, the reader will have noted, involves the expression of divine mysteries equally in all three Cosmic Realms or Regions. At the same time, however, the incarnational nature of Christianity emphasizes the living out or manifestation of these archetypal energies within the situations of daily life. In fact, the further one progresses along the path of the mysteries of the Son of Light, the more important is the way in which one approaches daily life in general. As is exemplified in the pattern of the Christ life, the most profound mysteries are sometimes "worked out" incognito and in the midst of apparently insignificant circumstances.

Even so, there can be little doubt that the oft referred to secret teachings given the Apostles by Christ included tuition on the descent and ascent of the soul through the various Regions and Planes. Not only did this tuition take the form of a "Book of the Dead" giving instruction for the passage of the soul after death, but quite obviously included teaching relating to the practice of "rising on the Planes." Paul, for instance, speaks of rising to the "third heaven." This teaching appears sporadically (it was, after all, secret) in texts such as the Ascension of Isaiah, the Apocalypse of Peter (which is contemporary with the Book of Revelation), and the Apocalypse of Paul. Such texts are not always easy to read, for their teachings about visionary ascent and descent through the Realms are often mixed with hellish stories of demons and damnation. In Magical Christianity, one learns to look beyond such negative images, seeing them for what they really are: largely deterrents or safeguards deliberately placed to discourage indiscriminate experience of the inner worlds by the uninitiated.

These safeguards are more the result of a spirit of compassionate protection rather than of any desire to exclude dedicated individuals from contacting the inner powers of the cosmos.

Behind these apocryphal tales is the visionary technique of rising on the Planes. This technique was partially assumed into Christianity through Jewish *Merkabah* esotericism—a forerunner of the Qabalah.

All this brings us once more to the diagram of the Qabalistic Tree (see figure 5). Most modern versions of the Tree show ten spheres indicating the relationships among various archetypal energies and states of being. On one level, these energies are expressed in terms of "planetary" spheres.

A similar designation was apparently in use in the early stages of Christian esotericism. Irenaeus writes of the three regions of "the heavens, the paradise and the city."[6] "The heavens" include the seven spheres of the visible planets and the *ogdoad*, or realm of the stars. These eight, when combined with "the paradise and the city" or New Jerusalem, yield a pattern of ten spheres. An alternative or extended view would be to see the paradise as the UnderRealm complement to the New Jerusalem, with the spheres as the ways and means of traversing the Realms. In this view the Terrestrial Realm becomes the point of manifestation for both the descending and ascending forces of creation. These powers are symbolized by the planets and stars of the

Figure 13. *The Magical Tree*

The Magical Tree is a flexible diagram used to show relationships among archetypal energies. It provides a means of orientation and a ground plan or itinerary for various forms of inner-plane journeys, meditations, and rituals. In the figure at left, the Terrestrial Realm is indicated by the central sphere, which shows a mountain and a cave—two features linking it to the Celestial and UnderRealm powers, respectively. The symbols of the planets shown in the upper half of the diagram also appear in the lower half as the symbols of the seven sacred metals. The planets and metals are correlated as follows: Moon = silver; Mercury = quicksilver, Venus = copper, Sun = gold, Mars = iron, Jupiter = tin, Saturn = lead. The spheres of the stars and the New Jerusalem in the Celestial Tree correspond to the spheres of the crystals and of Paradise in the UnderRealm Tree.

The higher or deeper aspects of each of the two Trees are, in this case, reached through the intercession of the Holy Virgin Mother as either Star Maiden or Black Madonna.

The figure below represents the Three Realms, the Two Trees, and the Egg of Creation.

Celestial Realm on one hand, and on the other by the seven ancient metals and the crystals of the UnderRealm (figure 13).

The actual technique of ascending through the spheres involves the assumption through ritual or vision of the spiritual qualities of each sphere successively. In Magical Christianity this is sometimes also expressed in terms of angelic beings or "states." Clement of Alexandria, for instance, says that the gnostic soul successively traverses the heavenly spheres, which correspond to the angelic orders. Taking on the form or state appropriate to the angelic nature of each sphere, the soul rises in contemplation until it achieves a lucid vision of the highest heaven.[7] In modern magical visions and ritual, one finds a complex interplay of symbolic correspondences. Usually the energies associated with each of the Three Realms are not worked with in their pure forms. Most magical practices employ symbols and energies drawn from all levels simultaneously. Normally, in other words, the Three Realms are worked together with varying degrees of emphasis on each one according to the structure and purpose of the meditation, ritual, or inner journey. Among other things this approach allows a more gradual and integrated passage through the relevant energies and experiences.

We give below two exercises that may be performed on alternating occasions. The first emphasizes the energies of the Celestial Realm; the second emphasizes certain positive elements of the UnderRealm experience. Both work through contact with the Holy Virgin Mother.

VISION EXERCISE ~ CD Track 7

Our Lady of the Stars

*A*fter beginning with the kenosis meditation, proceed as usual, reciting the appropriate phrases as you build up the symbols of the previous exercises: the Sphere of Creation, the Lance of Light, the Living Flame, the Sun Chalice.

As you say the ritual phrase for the next symbol, the Secret Gospels, the Chalice fills with light, which then spills over in a fourfold flash of light to the four directions.

You find yourself in the stone chapel, with each of its four walls dominated by a tall, massive, arched window filled with stained glass. You see the four closed books resting on stone lecterns, each facing one of the great windows.

You are standing facing the East and you notice near each corner of the wall a carved wooden door. The door near the right-hand corner attracts your attention because it has a lighted lamp hanging before it. You approach the door, which you see is carved with the patterns of the stars and the symbols of the planets. You take the lamp from its hook and with the other hand open the door. It swings inward and you see a winding stair leading up within the thick stone walls of the chapel. You ascend the stair and come out upon the roof of the chapel.

Breathing in the cool night air, you look around you and see to one side a stone shrine containing a magnificent statue of the Holy Virgin Mother. She is seated upon a throne of dark stone and has a veil and a cloak studded with stars. On her lap she holds an image of the Christ Child. In one hand the Child holds a globe with the celestial map engraved upon it. The other hand, raised in blessing, points toward the heavens.

You allow your gaze to move upward to the wondrous sea of stars in the sky above. There, standing in the heavens, you see a great figure of the Holy Virgin, Our Lady of the Stars. At her feet a dragon of rainbow light entwines itself about the polestar, writhing and undulating in flashes of variegated color.

From the outstretched hands of the Star Mother come threads of light that flash out among the stars, linking them into patterns that you recognize as the various constellations. And now into one hand she receives the seven rays of the seven ancient planets: an indigo ray of Saturn, a blue ray of Jupiter, a red ray of Mars, a golden ray of the Sun, a green ray of Venus, an orange ray of Mercury, and a silver ray of the Moon.

From her other hand, the purified rays of light descend to you, filling you with an intuitive awareness of deep cosmic principles: of the relationship between the shape and significance of the landscape and the patterns and power of the stars, as well as the meaning of the planets and their occult influence and relationship to your body and soul.

Having been baptized in these Celestial powers, you raise the lamp in salute to the Lady of the Stars, then kneel for a few moments in contemplation before the shrine of the Virgin and Child. You rise and make your way down the spiral stair to the chapel. You close the carved door and hang the lamp in its place.

The chapel fades from vision and you find yourself at the center of the star sphere. The sphere contracts, bringing the lights together until you are enclosed in an aura-sized globe of pure starlight. You become aware of the axis running through the poles of the sphere, of the golden flame within your heart, and of the chalice woven out of the light of the flame. The chalice fills with light, which when it reaches the rim, spills over in a great lightning flash to the four directions.

And now, become aware, just above your head, of a shining crown of seven stars. And as you meditate upon the meaning of this symbol, recite the relevant ceremonial phrase (suggestions: "a starry crown of seven rays," "blessed are those who touch the stars," or "be hallowed by a starry crown").

VISION EXERCISE ⌣ *CD Track 8*

Our Lady of the Crystals

*A*fter the kenosis meditation, proceed as usual, reciting the
appropriate phrases as you build up the symbols of the previous exercises: the Sphere of Creation, the Lance of Light, the
Living Flame, and the Sun Chalice.

As you say the ritual phrase for the next symbol, the Secret
Gospels, the Chalice fills with light, which then spills over in a
fourfold flash of light to the four directions.

You are again in the stone chapel looking toward the eastern
wall. This time, you notice that the lamp hangs over the door near
the left-hand corner. Approaching the door, which is inset with
gems and precious metals, you take the lamp from its peg. You open
the door and pass onto a stair that winds downward into the earth.

You come out into a dark cave or crypt beneath the chapel.
To one side you see a shrine containing a statue of a Black Virgin
and Child. Their golden robes are studded with gems and crystals. The image of the Child has in one hand a crystal sphere
etched with geometric patterns, while the other hand points downward in blessing. You follow the direction with your vision and see
at the foot of the shrine, safeguarded by a wrought-iron grill in
the form of a vesica piscis, a deep well or fissure in the earth.
You lower your lamp and look into the well.

The light reflects from a myriad of shining crystals that flash
like a sea of stars in the great cavern beneath you.

Amid the light of the crystals forms a figure of the Holy
Virgin, Our Lady of the Crystals. Beneath her feet a rainbow
dragon undulates in flashes of variegated light. The Virgin
extends her arms, sending out threads of light into the earth itself,

weaving the crystals together in the pattern of a great latticework of energy flowing through the very fabric of the land. You realize that the points where the threads of the lattice of light join together mark the locations of all sacred sites throughout the world.

And now, into one hand, the Mother draws the energy of the seven sacred metals: an indigo ray of lead, a blue ray of tin, a red ray of iron, a golden ray of gold, a green ray of copper, an orange ray of quicksilver, and a silver ray of silver. Then from her other hand, a pure light shoots upward, filling you with deep cosmic awareness of the principles of creation and existence. These, you realize, are active and accessible within the land and within your body and soul.

Having been bathed in this fountain of energy, you move your lamp in salute to the Virgin and then kneel briefly in contemplation before the shrine of the Mother and Child. You rise and return up the spiral stair to the chapel. As you close the door and hang the lamp in its place, the chapel fades from vision.

You are once again at the center of the cosmic sphere. The sphere contracts, bringing the stars together until you are encompassed by an aura-sized globe of starlight. You are aware of the axis running through the poles of the sphere and of the golden flame within your heart. Out of the light of the flame appears the chalice. This itself fills with light, which, when it reaches the rim, spills over in a great lightning flash to the four directions.

Above your head you are aware of the shining crown of seven stars. And now you become aware, in complement to the crown, of a great crystal throbbing with power in the earth beneath your feet. As you meditate upon the meaning of the symbols, you recite the appropriate ritual phrase (suggestions: "a crystal stone of sure foundation," "blessed are those who find the stone," or "be hallowed by a crystal stone").

The ℙLANES *of* 𝔅EING

he concept of a three-tiered universe is found in nearly all spiritual traditions and has many forms and nuances. The pattern of the Three Realms is one of these. It is one that fits, however, into the much larger pattern of the Planes of Being. This pattern consists of the Material or Physical Plane, the Intermedial or Psychic Plane, and the Spiritual or Archetypal Plane (figures 14 and 15). These three planes resonate with the threefold constitution of the human being. The Material Plane correlates with the physical body, the Psychic Plane with the soul, and the Archetypal Plane with the spirit. We might further link the planes and the human constitution with three modes of perception. The purely material level corresponds to sensation and to discursive or analytical reason. The Psychic Plane corresponds to the inner, psychic, or prophetic senses, to symbolic thinking, and to what is often called the creative imagination. The Archetypal Plane corresponds to higher modes of philosophical thought, to mystical apprehension, and to spiritual intuition. Let us look in more detail at each of the planes.

Figure 14. *The Planes of Being*

*This illustration shows the Planes of Being conceived of as spheres within spheres.
The Fourth World or Plane of Being—beyond all Planes, yet simultaneously
encompassing, permeating, and generating the whole of creation—is Deity, which
is vari-ously depicted here as (a) Ultimate Being: that which epitomizes all being;
(b)Infinite Being: that which embraces all being; and (c)Non-Being: that
which is beyond all being.*

The Material Plane deals with sensory facts, with physical objects,
with the use of reason to draw inference from sensory data. Viewed
from the flatland of its own level, the Physical Plane embodies a perspective that determines reality solely in quantitative terms. This is the
position of reductive materialist science or "scientism," as it is sometimes called. There is, from this point of view, an attempt to reduce

reality to biological terms and corresponding a tendency to view the world as mechanistic and meaningless and to see human life as devoid of any higher or deeper significance or interpretation. The scientistic experience tends to awaken the characteristics of narrowness, materialism, greed, and a general disdain for one's fellows (who are, after all, merely objects, or randomly "evolved" organisms in a purposeless world). In other words, the mere material perspective spawns an essentially soulless existence without design or meaning.

Unfortunately this is fast becoming the standard mode of perception for people in the modern West. Relatively few people nowadays

Figure 15. *The Planes of Being, the Two Trees, and the Three Realms*
Only the highest and deepest levels of the Tree touch upon the Archetypal Plane, here symbolized by a circle of abstract figures.

admit the existence of the Psychic Plane. And the Spiritual Plane is generally consigned a vague, distant significance—one considered hardly relevant for life in the "real world" except perhaps to be touted as a "source" for literal-minded moralism or rigid behavioral precepts. No matter how strongly its existence is denied, however, the two thirds of creation corresponding to the Psychic and Archetypal Planes will not be ignored. Thus one sees in modern society the irruption of the "New Age" movements. Though these appear generally spurious or superficial to serious practitioners of traditional magical arts, they nonetheless serve to reconnect popular consciousness to inner reality—albeit in a tenuous, incomplete, camouflaged, or even degenerate manner. But even a thin and dangerously frayed thread of connection is better than none at all.

One of the reasons the Spiritual Plane seems so inaccessible to many people is their disavowal of the reality of the Psychic or Intermedial Plane. "The structure of reality is such that it is not possible to move from one end to the other unless one passes through the middle," wrote Thomas Aquinas.[1] The Psychic Plane is the middle plane, the plane of mediation. It allows us simultaneously to reach both towards spiritual reality and the physical environment in meaningful ways. Those who learn to operate from this plane find that it transfigures the material reality, imbuing it with depth, meaning, and power. Certain features of the landscape, certain aspects of architecture, certain areas of the human physiology assume an occult significance and connectedness, becoming portals to unseen energies and realities. The Psychic Plane ensouls the Physical Plane, and by it the great web of nature is vivified. Through it the various kingdoms of nature—mineral, vegetative, and animal—become active and significant. It is thus the plane of the totem animals, of herbal correspondences, of healing stones, and the like. It is approached through the inner senses, through mythic and symbolic thought and perception. It deals with unseen forces and "spiritual" beings, with prophecy, vision, psychic abilities, and occult powers.

Primarily a plane of symbols and energies, the Psychic Plane is characterized, among other things, by a certain fluidity. It has its own structure and principles, but these are not of such a nature as to yield their secrets to mechanical or quantitative observation. It is closely connected to our ability to understand the Three Realms that were the subject of chapter 6: the Terrestrial Realm or transfigured Physical Plane,[2] which has both a visible and invisible aspect; the Celestial Realm, which deals with visionary symbolism of an ascensional nature; and the UnderRealm, which deals with visions of a descensional nature. Those who actively engage the Psychic Plane inevitably find themselves in contact with "inner" beings of various kinds. There are generally three types of beings one might encounter on this plane: those that are beneficial to the human soul, those that are neutral to human well-being, and those that are inimical to humanity. Clearly the forces of the Psychic Plane should not to be invoked indiscriminately, that is, without proper orientation, guidance, and protection.[3]

For obvious reasons the mystery traditions of the world tend to concern themselves primarily with those inner plane contacts that have the well-being of humanity at heart or that can benefit from positive contact with human consciousness: masters, saints, heroes, goddesses and gods, figures from myth and legend and historical figures whose lives carried archetypal patterns, bodhisattvas, devas, power animals, faeries, elementals, angels—and the list goes on.

Before considering some of the beings that play a role in esoteric Christian tradition, it will be useful to look at the subject of beneficent inner-plane contacts from a general perspective. One way to do this is by considering the various beings in terms of their spiritual function or role. We may say, then, that some beings operate primarily as guides, some as guardians, and some as mediators.[4]

Inner guides are characterized by their concern with communication between the planes. They invariably offer some form of useful message or teaching. They are the inner teachers, counselors, and wayshowers. The actual process of communication may take various forms. It may involve mediumship, where the physical body is temporarily given over to the control of an inner guide. Or it may work through the perceptions of the inner senses. One might for instance "hear" the teaching or see an inner guide in vision. Or one might simply sense the presence of a guide and then pay particular attention to thoughts, images, and ideas that happen to arise in the mind. These may then be translated into verbal or visual form. Alternatively, a guide could appear in the inner vision to take one upon a magical journey. In this case the message might be encoded in the symbolism of the images and experience itself. Sometimes, communication occurs through meaningful coincidence, or "signs following." This way of listening to a guide involves paying attention to the inherent symbolism of certain happenings in daily life, intuitively deciphering from them relevant teaching and guidance.

Guardians are beings who preserve and protect human beings, sacred sites, secret teachings, and holy mysteries. There are many levels or aspects to the role of guardianship. There are, on one hand, those beings whose function it is to protect people either individually (i.e., one-to-one) or collectively (on the basis of individuals' association with a sacred site, temple, lodge, or magical order).

On the other hand, inner guardian beings are also involved in protecting sacred sites and ritual workings from disturbance by the curious or unworthy. In mystery rituals, the guardian being (or beings) is closely associated with the office of doorkeeper.

The doorkeeper role is a special commission that hinges on the development of a particular relationship between the soul of the individual who holds the office and the guardian spirit of the lodge.

Sacred sites have always had their *genii locorum*, their guardian spirits. Although modern man's estrangement from the Psychic Plane has left the landscape relatively impoverished in terms of acknowledged sacred sites, there are some sites where guardians are still active and many others where they are merely dormant. For this reason, discretion is required when visiting some of these sites, even where they may seem to have degenerated into little more than benign tourist attractions.

The guardians' power to deter has much to do with what used to be called "glamor." Glamor is in some ways similar to the modern notion of "psychological projection" in that it involves beholding in others a reflection of the unacknowledged aspects of our own souls. So far as the warding energies sometimes contacted at sacred sites are concerned, this reflection usually involves the unredeemed or negative elements of oneself. This encounter can be quite the disturbing experience it is meant to be, for it usually affects relationships with those whom one holds dear or who are otherwise closely connected to the activities of one's daily life. Family, friends, career, or employment relationships are the usual pegs upon which is hung the mirror of psychic glamor. As we noted in chapter 6, the same process is behind what is known in the mystery teachings as facing the Dweller on the Threshold—a fearsome entity who traditionally stands at the portal of initiation, guarding the passage from the lesser to the greater mysteries. Although active on several levels beyond that of personal psychology, the Dweller is commonly considered to embody the negative aggregate of one's soul. Facing or passing the Dweller on the Threshold requires that we accept, sublimate, or redeem the unbalanced aspects of ourselves. This step can be relatively easy or hard depending on the aspirant's courage, integrity, and willingness to change.

It will be noted from this discussion that guardians in general are very much concerned with maintaining the distinction between sacred and profane. This distinction does not occur primarily in objects or places themselves, but in the attitudes and spiritual integrity of those who would approach sacred matters: *Hekas, hekas, estoi babeloi!* resounds the opening of the ancient mysteries—"Begone, profane ones!"

Mediators are inner beings who are concerned with aiding in the mediation of unseen forces and inner energies between the Three Realms and the Planes of Being. They inevitably work in concert with incarnate humans to enable the relay of archetypal and ultimately beneficent forces and patterns from the inner planes into the sphere of human consciousness and activity. They are the great beings associated with healing, both of individuals and of groups, even up to the level of planetary healing.

Mediators play an important role in high magical ritual. Technically speaking, magical ritual involves setting up inner conduits through which spiritual power is enabled to flow from one plane of reality of another. This is why ritual work, properly understood, always builds upon a general symbolic pattern representing simultaneously the spiritual structure of the cosmos and the constitution of the human being. The pattern of correspondences thus laid down enables mediation to take place. Mediation occurs through the principle of resonance or attunement. A particular sequence of symbols, built up in the inner vision,[5] enables consciousness to "vibrate" at a certain level, thus becoming a potential channel for the energies of that level.

Like guardians, mediators are sometimes associated with sacred sites. But whereas guardians are there to keep unwanted influences out and desired ones safe, mediators are concerned with enabling a flow of energy to take place within the protected confines of sacred space. Let us recall that our division of beings into guides, guardians, and mediators is based upon relationships between inner beings and incarnate humans. Specific entities may therefore function variously, or even simultaneously, in all three "orders." We shall see examples of this shortly.

In ancient and magical Christianity, the orders of beings who perform the functions of guides, guardians, and mediators are encountered in various forms, including the angelic hierarchies, the Virgin Mary, the saints and martyrs, animal beings, and ultimately the Christ. It is the Son of Light in whom all being is subsumed and who therefore generates and epitomizes the roles of guide, guardian, and mediator. Similarly, the Virgin Mary bears the titles of Mediatrix or Intercessor, Protector, and Guide. To a lesser degree the archangels also embody the functions of all three orders. Michael, for instance, is guide as psychopomp, guardian as the angel before the gate of paradise, and mediator as the presence presiding over the powers of a vast network of holy places. It is perhaps in reference to an archangel or to a "guardian angel" that the fourth century writer Synesius of Cyrene directs the following hymn: "And give me a companion, O King, a partner, a sacred messenger of sacred power, a messenger of prayer illumined by the divine light, a friend, a dispenser of noble gifts, a guard of my soul, a guard of my life, a guard over prayers, a guard over deeds."[6]

It was common in ancient Christianity for saints to appear as inner guides to select individuals.[7] Gregory Thaumaturgus, for instance, mentions being guided and nurtured by an inner presence. The Christian poet, bishop, and imperial arbitrator Paulinus of Nola frequently received guidance from the spirit of Saint Felix.[8]

Accounts of intercession of the martyred saints are also numerous. In the case of the martyrs, who carried on the ancient traditions of heroes and sacred kings, their power of intercession was closely linked to the sanctuaries or *martyria* that housed their remains. The heroic saints were believed to be somehow merged with their sacred sites. Their holy presence, being both immediate and transcendent, enabled them to function as mediatory beings between divine reality and terrestrial human life. This powerful intercessory experience came eventually to be applied to the saints in general, not just the martyrs. And so it became important that every altar be founded upon the relics of a saint.

As the traditions of the communion of saints spread through Christendom, certain magical practices developed alongside them. Until the end of the Middle Ages, for instance, people commonly engaged in *incubation*, which involved sleeping inside a sanctuary or church to receive healing and guidance given in a dream vision of the patron saint.[9]

In addition to the saints and martyrs, angelic beings play an important part in magical Christian practice. They are particularly important for the role they play in the techniques of "rising on the planes." The traditions of angelic hierarchies were first crystallized in written form by a sixth-century initiate who wrote under the name of Dionysios the Areopagite.

For Dionysios there are nine angelic orders divided into three triads of three orders each. Interestingly, these triads correspond to the three Planes of Being. The lower triad of principalities, archangels, and angels corresponds to the Physical Plane; the middle triad of dominions, powers, and authorities corresponds to the Psychic Plane; The upper triad of seraphim, cherubim, and thrones corresponds with the Archetypal Plane.

According to Dionysios, each of the triads also expresses a corresponding spiritual process. The principalities, archangels, and angels rule over the process of purification. The dominions, powers, and authorities preside over the process of illumination. The seraphim, cherubim, and thrones rule over the process of perfection.[10]

We have in all this the outline of a tradition of spiritual development that hinges on relationships between angelic beings and human consciousness. The intermediary assistance of angelic beings and of symbolic visions is necessary for our spiritual growth, says Dionysios, because "we lack the ability to be directly raised up to conceptual contemplations."[11] This brings us to the Archetypal Plane.

The Archetypal Plane has to do with essences, universals, and holisms, with ideals, virtues, and spiritual principles. It is the plane of what are generally called the "divine names." The divine names or attributes, then, are universal principles, or archetypes. Following a Qabalistic formula, one pattern of archetypal principles might be perfection, wisdom, understanding, love, justice, beauty, power, glory, strength, and unity. None of these can be apprehended by human mentation or imagination, except "as in a glass, darkly."

Only through contemplation or spiritual intuition can the universals be grasped in any real fashion. And even then it is quite impossible to express the experience, except imperfectly through spiritual conduct or symbolic imagery. Even the so-called *via negativa* which claims to reject all images as inadequate, cannot escape expressing itself through images—though they be images of darkness, emptiness, a dark cloud, and so on—all of which symbolize an experience or reality that cannot otherwise be expressed. Thus again we see the mediatory importance of the Psychic Plane, this time as a means of access to the plane of archetypal ideas or essences.

Each plane can be said to encompass or transfigure the plane or planes below it. We saw how the Physical Plane is encountered in a more meaningful way when viewed from the psychic level of experience. So too are the Physical Plane and Psychic Planes transformed when vision has been washed in the pool of archetypal experience. The Physical Plane carries thenceforth not only a psychic significance, but also a spiritual dimension.

There are certain types of holy places, sacred images, or spiritual beings whose importance derives from their common participation in an archetype (that is in their universal essence on the

Archetypal Plane). All gods for instance, tend toward the One God (this is Abba—the High Father—not to be confused with the Ultimate Deity), all goddesses toward the Great Goddess, all nodes or centers toward the Cosmic Center, all axial images towards the Universal Axis, and so on. It is a realization of this resonant property of creation that prompts the fifteenth-century cardinal and mystical philosopher Nicholas of Cusa to remark of the ancient pagans, "they adored the Divinity in all the gods."[12] And Gregory of Palamas speaks of the transformed vision of those who have been "deified" or "divinized": "Miraculously, they see with a sense that exceeds the senses, and with a mind that exceeds mind, for the power of the spirit penetrates their human faculties, and allows them to see things which are beyond us."[13]

Moreover, the transformation of perception experienced in each of the Planes of Being involves a corresponding transfiguration in the appropriate layers of the human constitution. On the Psychic Plane the hidden powers of the soul are reflected in the occult anatomy. On the Archetypal Plane spiritual energies are reflected in the mystical physiology of the human being.

Quoting Palamas again: "In spiritual man, the grace of the Spirit, transmitted to the body through the soul, grants to the body also the experience of things divine...."[14]

All this ties in with the esoteric doctrine of "centers," which teaches the significance of certain areas of the physical body as focal points for occult and spiritual energies. The activation and unfoldment of the magical powers of the soul and the granting of the Gifts of the Spirit, lies behind the secret teaching on the "resurrection body." We are speaking of the transfiguration, deification, or redemption of the human being on all levels—and this not as an eschatological hope, as in the exoteric doctrines, but as an immediate experience available to the initiate *hic et nunc*.

Successive experience of each of the Planes of Being brings the initiate closer to Ultimate Being, which might be termed the "Fourth Plane," the Plane that contains, generates, and enables all others. That is, each plane is qualitatively higher than the one below it. In other words it more closely approaches or embodies completion, wholeness, and therefore holiness. The "lower" planes are never left behind, but they are transfigured.

The fall of humanity constitutes estrangement from the primordial wholeness of the Edenic state. The redemption of humankind means restoration to a life lived from the Spiritual Plane. Then shall "the very God of peace sanctify you wholly . . . spirit, soul and body" (1 Thess. 5:23).

VISION EXERCISE ⟿ *CD Track 9*

The Litany of Light

*T*he exercise given below comprises a ritual synthesis of the concourse of energies evoked through the practical work of the previous chapters. It works something like a magical rosary or chaplet.

Indeed, in addition to collecting seven candles for this exercise, it might be useful to construct or purchase a chaplet of seven (or a multiple of seven) beads as an enhancement to the exercise. Observe that the exercise is built upon the suggested ritual phrases that were given at the end of each of the preceeding chapters.

The litany is composed of several sections: opening and closing invocations bracket an evocation of the seven symbols, a set of beatitudes, and a hallowing sequence. Operational notes on the various sections follow the text of the litany.

Litany

{light central candle}
Let there be Light.
{raise right hand above head, then touch forehead}
In the name of the High Father,
{touch navel}
And of the Deep Mother,
{touch left shoulder, then right shoulder}
And of the Son of Light,
{bring palms together before heart}
One Light, One Life, One Eternal Spirit.
Amen

May Being be blessed and sanctified
by this chaplet of seven sacred symbols:
A shining sphere of cosmic love,
Amen
A piercing ray of deepest peace,
Amen
A holy fount of living fire,
Amen
A chalice in the sacred heart,
Amen
A turning cross of life unfolding,
Amen
A starry crown of seven rays,
Amen
A crystal stone of sure foundation,
Amen
Upon the Way of Light.

Blessed are those who are centered in Love,

For theirs is the Kingdom of Light. {*light candle 1*}
Blessed are those transfixed by Peace,
For theirs is the Kingdom of Light. {*light candle 2*}
Blessed are those who raise up the Fire,
For theirs is the Kingdom of Light. {*light candle 3*}
Blessed are those who seek the Grail,
For theirs is the Kingdom of Light. {*light candle 4*}
Blessed are those upon the Cross,
For theirs is the Kingdom of Light. {*light candle 5*}
Blessed are those who touch the Stars,
For theirs is the Kingdom of Light. {*light candle 6*}
Blessed are those who find the Stone,
For theirs is the Kingdom of Light. {*light candle 7*}

Be hallowed by a sacred sphere,
Be hallowed by a piercing ray,
Be hallowed by a living fire,
Be hallowed by a holy grail,
Be hallowed by a turning cross,
Be hallowed by a starry crown,
Be hallowed by a crystal stone,
Upon the Path of Peace.

{*raise right hand above head then touch forehead*}
In the name of the High Father,
{*touch navel*}
And of the Deep Mother,
{*touch left shoulder, then right shoulder*}
And of the Living Son of Light,
{*bring palms together before heart*}
One Light, One Life, One Eternal Spirit.
Amen

Notes on the Exercise

Opening and Closing Invocation. This portion of the ritual may be accompanied by the visualization of a cross of light with a rosy flame at its center. The invocation of the High Father and Deep Mother serves to direct the spiritual will towards the ultimate resolution of opposites. This is done by presenting the spiritual paradox that height is equivalent to depth and is ritually signified by the marking and visualization of a vertical axis of infinite length.

The term "Son of Light" is an ancient title of Christ appearing, among other places, in certain Syriac traditions of the Magi and the birth of Christ. Within these traditions the light is of the Archetypal Plane and its manifestation or theophany is at the center of the story of the Star of Bethlehem. The breaking through of the Archetypal Light to the Physical Plane is signified by envisioning and ritually drawing a horizontal ray of light passing though one's heart. The invocation of the Spirit and the envisioning of a rosy flame in the heart signify the unification or joining of the vertical and horizontal "polarities" of the cross of light.

Evocation of the Seven Symbols. This portion of the litany is an initial building up of the symbols of the previous chapters. The word "Amen," meaning simply "let it be" or "let it be so," should be slowly intoned, as it incorporates certain ancient sonic principles of mediation and manifestation.

The Beatitudes. These are based upon the ritual rhythms inherent in the Beatitudes of the Sermon on the Mount. Again, the seven symbols are evoked. As the rubrics of the litany indicate, a candle may be lit for each of the Beatitudes. One might therefore arrange upon one's work space or altar a central white candle within a circle of seven candles of the colors of the spectrum. These could then be lighted in sequence.

The Hallowing. The hallowing or "making holy" is the third level of a three-stage consecration of consciousness inherent in the litany. It is a simple and powerful expression of the spiritual will.

The MIRYAM TRADITION

In the history of authoritarian or institutionalized Christianity, the power of the divine feminine was rarely recognized, less often understood, and pretty much never accepted. We do glimpse it, however, in the early doctrine of the Holy Spirit; in the *Theotokos* and *Hagia Sophia* of the Eastern church; and in the Marianic mysteries of the medieval Western church.

Outside of conventional theology we find it at the foundations of medieval movements such as the troubadours and the *Fedeli d'Amore*. It is in the flowering of the Grail stories, and at the center of the work of initiates such as Dante Alighieri. It is in the holy books of early Gnostics, and in the popular legends and lore of many later Christian communities worldwide. And it is at the heart of the Rosicrucian movement so prominent in seventeenth-century Europe.

However, the feminine power runs most strongly through Magical Christianity in what must be called the Miryam tradition. In conventional Christianity, Miryam is generally considered a minor Old Testament figure, known at best as Moses's somewhat troublesome sister. However, as we will see, Miryam first embodies and then (re)generates a stream of initiatory, mystical, and prophetic power that flows into a group of New Testament women named Miryam (or Mary, to use the anglicized form of the name).[1]

MIRYAM AS HOLY SPIRIT

For many with Christian backgrounds, a helpful way to get an initial grasp on the power that enables the Miryam tradition is to say it is of the Holy Spirit. The Christian doctrine of the Holy Spirit was influenced by ancient Hebrew traditions of the *Ruach* and, later, the *Shekinah*. The words *ruach* and *shekinah* are both feminine and refer to the divine spirit and holy presence, respectively.

Ruach is the spirit that hovered like a bird over the divine void (Gen. 1:2). This association with the bird likely influenced Christian images of the Holy Spirit as a dove. The dove, of course, is the attribute of many ancient goddesses. Of particular interest here are the Sumerian Inanna, her Babylonian counterpart Ishtar, and their Canaanite cognates Anat and Astarte.

In Ugaritic mythology, Anat/Astarte, the Canaanite Goddess of war, sexuality, and fertility (and probably of the moon) was often merged or confused with Asherah, who was originally a goddess of the waters, and later of the Tree of Life. Both Ashereh and Anat seem to be consorts of the Canaanite High God. This connection is interesting because we find references to "Yahweh and his Asherah" in inscriptions at Kuntillet Ajrud in the Sinai desert, and to "Anat-Yahweh" (or Anat-Yahu) at an ancient Jewish sanctuary at Elephantine, Egypt.[2] These suggest in the first case a goddess-consort of Yahweh, and in the second the fusion of Yahweh with the Canaanite goddess of war. Anat, in particular, has characteristics highly reminiscent of Durga-Kali, the Hindu goddess of destruction and regeneration.[3]

Equally important in the history of the Holy Spirit is the *Shekinah*, which, according to the Talmud, is a comforting presence that brings joy in the midst of travails. But it is also the dark whirling cloud that leads the Israelites through the desert of the Exodus, and at the same time, the irresistible power that inspires creativity and prophetic utterance.[4] In Qabalistic teaching (i.e., Zohar 1:223 a–b), the *Shekinah* is closely associated with the moon, just as the Holy Spirit is associated with the moon in Christian esoteric tradition. (It is said that the moon's orbit marks the sphere of influence of the Holy Spirit as it plays upon the earth.)

The moon's resonance with woman, water, and with the rhythms of birth, life, death, and the seasons, plays an important role in many archaic cultures and spiritual practices. In common with most ancient peoples in the Middle East, the Hebrews used a lunar calendar, which was closely connected to planting and harvesting rhythms. This is interesting because Solomon's Temple was built on a threshing floor (2 Sam. 24:21 ff).

The Hebrew word for threshing floor, *goren*, also means "place of the void," possibly referring to the dark cloud of chaff that rises when wheat is threshed, but simultaneously suggesting the dark cloud of Exodus and its connections to the *Shekinah* and the Void. Ancient threshing floors in the Levant often contained shrines to the divinities of the harvest. Evidence in the Ugaritic texts of Ras Shamra suggests that likely candidates for these in Canaanite tradition are Anat or Mot, or both.[5] David too, builds an altar to the Lord on the threshing floor that would be the site of Solomon's Temple (2 Sam. 24). It is not surprising, then, to learn that Solomon's Temple was dedicated on or near the autumnal equinox, a time strongly associated with the themes of fruition and harvest.

A whole complex of powerful feminine images intersects at the threshing floor: void, moon, goddess, *Shekinah*, dark cloud, temple. This can be seen as a development or harmonic of an earlier confluence of feminine power and presence at the crossing of the Red Sea, where Miryam prophesies, sings, and dances victoriously before the Pillar of Cloud (*Shekinah*). Among the ancient Israelites, the parting of the Red Sea was recognized as a spiritual harmonic of the parting of the waters by the *Ruach* at the Creation.[6]

This feminine power streams through later Judaic tradition and into Christianity, where it is embodied in the women who make up the Miryam tradition.[7] While there is only one significant figure named Miryam in the Old Testament, the New Testament speaks of a number of Miryams. The Miryams or Marys are prominent not only at key places and events in the stories of the New Testament, but also in certain Gnostic and apocryphal books, as well as in esoteric legend and lore right down to the present day. Let's look at these figures.

MIRYAM THE PROPHETESS

The sister of Moses is a unique and important figure in Judeo-Christian tradition. She appears in Exodus as the first prophetess, and she dances before the dark pillar of cloud, singing songs of war. In the Old Testament, the name Miryam is significantly connected only to this figure (Exod. 15; Num. 12, 20, 26; Deut. 24; 1 Chron. 6; Mic. 6). Her name probably means "bitter" or "rebellious."[8]

In biblical and legendary tradition she is linked especially to water: She hides her baby brother Moses by the river in Egypt; she sings a battle song, the Song of the Sea, when the Egyptian army is drowned in the Red Sea; and from the Tosefta there is the legend about the Well of Miryam that followed the Israelites on the Exodus but dried up at her death.

In esoteric teaching she is the exemplar and archetypal founder of the Miryam tradition.[9]

THE NINE MARYS

The New Testament presents nine more or less distinct figures named Mary (though Salome only becomes Mary Salome in apocryphal works); the relevant passages are listed in table 2. From a practical inner point of view they can be envisioned as a sisterhood of priest-esses or prophetesses (or sibyls, as they were called in the Roman world) who surrounded Jesus and were an active force in early Christianity. In the following discussion, the Nine Marys are num-bered primarily for clarity and convenience. However, there is a rough correlation between the number sequence and the relative importance of the figures, so that, generally speaking, the higher the number, the greater the depth of tradition surrounding that Mary.

Table 2. *Sources for the Nine Marys*

1. Mary of Rome	Rom. 16:6
2. Mary the Hostess	Acts 12:12
3. Mary Cleopas (or Clopas)	John 19:25
	Luke 24:18
4. The Other Mary	Matt. 27:61
5. Mary Jacobe	Matt. 27:56
	Mark 15:40, 15:47
6. Mary of Bethany	Luke 10:38–42
	John 11:1–5, 11:17–20, 11:28–33, 12:1–8
7. Mary of Magdala	Matt. 27:55–56, 27:61, 28:1
	Mark 15:40–41, 15:47, 16:1, 16:9
	Luke 8:2, 24:10
	John 19:25, 20:1, 20:11, 20:16, 20:18
8. Mary Salome	Mark 15:40, 16:1
9. Mary of Nazareth	Matt. 1–2, 11:46–50, 13:53–58
	Mark 3:31–35, 6:3–4
	Luke 1–2, 3:23, 4:16–30, 8:19–21, 11:28–29
	John 2:1–12, 6:42, 19:25–27
	Acts 1:14
	Rom. 1–3
	Gal. 4:4

1. Mary of Rome. This Mary is a leader and spiritual worker in an early Roman community. She is the first of four women to be thanked at the end of Paul's Epistle to the Romans. The letter is significant because it mentions a number of esoteric themes in connection with the community in which Mary took a leading role. Among these are

- The power of grace (*charis*), which has connections to the *Shekinah*, the power that enables prophetic utterance (Rom. 10:6–7).

- The spiritual technique of the Armor of Light, which appears to be a taking on of the power of Torah or the Word (Rom. 13:11 ff; see also Eph. 6:13–17).

- A secret teaching or mystery (Rom. 16:25).

2. Mary the Hostess. In medieval tradition, she was hostess of the house of the Upper Room,[10] which links her to the mysteries of the Grail through the blood and body of Christ. In later Christian Qabalistic teaching, the Upper Room is located at the edge of the Void (*Da'ath*).

3. Mary Cleopas (or Clopas). This Mary is closely connected to a couple of the central mysteries of Christ's life, appearing at the Crucifixion with Mary of Magdala and Mary of Nazareth and also as one of the first witnesses to Jesus's Resurrection. Mary Cleopas is sometimes identified with Mary of Nazareth, and sometimes with Salome.

4. The Other Mary. This Mary is mentioned as one of the women at the tomb and is thus connected to the deepest mysteries of Christ's Descent to the UnderRealm. She is often identified with Mary Jacobe and sometimes with Salome.

5. Mary Jacobe. This Mary is the mother of the apostle James the Less. She was with Mary of Magdala at the Crucifixion and with Salome at Jesus's tomb in order to anoint the body of Jesus. She is sometimes identified with Mary Cleopas or Mary of Nazareth.

She is also significant in later tradition as one of the Marys who sailed to France with other figures important in esoteric Christian tradition, including Joseph of Arimethea, Lazarus, and Sara the Egyptian.

6. Mary of Bethany. Often identified with Mary of Magdala, Mary of Bethany is the sister of Lazarus (whose traditions contain strong initiatory elements, namely, death, revivication, passing of a secret teaching, and so on).

This Mary is herself associated with a ritual of empowerment in which she anoints Jesus's feet and dries them with her hair. Various modern authors have drawn parallels between this and ancient Near Eastern marriage rites and the anointing of kings. In any case, the internal symbolic structure of the episode is magically significant: Oil is traditionally a vehicle of magical power, while, among other things, hair binds, seals, or controls it. The sequence presents some interesting practical possibilities, and it would not be difficult to develop exercises based on the pattern as a way of opening up, enhancing, and protecting personal visionary abilities.

7. Mary of Magdala. Widely fashionable now, Mary of Magdala has transformed in the popular mind from repentant whore to Grail-bearing wife of Jesus and mother of his child. It is important to realize that despite a lack of historical evidence, these trends express powerful inner dynamics that are entirely valid in their own context.

For nearly two thousand years, Mary of Magdala has been associated with themes that are esoteric and initiatory. We can cite everything from the symbolic significance of her association with the red egg in Eastern Christianity (see chapter 1), to the Gnostic traditions that present her as Jesus's companion and suggested sexual partner (though this character is even more evident in the figure of Salome; see below) and thus first among the Apostles, to her rivalry with Peter, to her relatively modern incarnation as a bearer of the bloodline of the Grail.

Equally significant is the canonical vision of her as a central figure in the stories of Jesus that most closely fit the initiatory paradigm of death, descent, rebirth (i.e., the Crucifixion, Entombment, and Resurrection).

As an inner figure, she embodies an important stream or current of power. She is very much the bearer of a new seed, a child, one might say. And that child is crucial to the regeneration of Christianity as a meaningful initiatory tradition.

8. Mary Salome. Salome is an underrated and enigmatic figure, strongly associated with the mysteries of the Dark Goddess. In canonical lore she is present at Jesus's crucifixion and is one of the women at the tomb. But it is her roles in apocryphal lore that mark her most strongly as an important figure in the esoteric Christian tradition.

In certain Gnostic circles she was identified with Salome, the dancer who asked for the head of John the Baptist (Mark 6:21–29). Among the Carpocrations and other early sects, she was held to be the transmitter of a secret doctrine.[11] And in the Gospel of Thomas she appears as sexual initiatrix[12] and esoteric questioner (verse 61):

> Jesus said, "Two will rest on a bed: the one will die, and the other will live."
>
> Salome said, "Who are you, man, that you . . . have come up on my couch and eaten from my table?"
>
> Jesus said to her, "I am he who exists from the undivided."

Her presence in Thomas is surely made more poignant when we realize that Salome in the Miryam tradition parallels the role of Thomas in the apostolic tradition. In the Protevangelion of James,[13] Salome has much the same relation to Mary as Thomas has to Jesus in the New Testament episode of the doubter. Just as Thomas makes intimate contact with the wound in the side of the resurrected Christ, so Salome, a midwife, makes contact with Mary of Nazareth at Jesus's birth, touching her hymen to see if she was truly virgin.

Salome's connection with the Dark Goddess (whose mysteries are those of birth, death, and regeneration), is played up in a couple of other ways too. Her name, for instance, seems to be related to *Shulamite*, which links her to the mystical eroticism of the Song of Solomon (6:13). The central character of the Song of Solomon is also often identified with the Queen of Sheba, who herself embodies a line of esoteric realization with powerful currents connected to sexual mysteries, especially as these relate to interrelations between humans and the faery-like beings known in Arabic tradition as *jinn*.

It is also worth mentioning one other sense in which Salome links with Dark Goddess traditions. Salome is one of the three Marys who travel with Joseph of Arimethea to Europe after the death of Jesus. With her in the boat is her servant Sara, known to Roma peoples as

Sara la Kali—Black Sara—and revered as their patron saint. Every year thousands of Roma visit her shrine in the crypt of Saintes Maries de la Mer in southern France.

9. Mary of Nazareth. Mary of Nazareth is of course the most prominent and best-known figure in the Miryam tradition, as mother of Jesus (in Eastern Orthodox tradition, mother of God) and leader of the Apostles, a tremendous amount of lore and legend has accumulated around her. I have dealt briefly with some of this material in chapter 6, especially as she is imagined as Star Maiden and Deep Mother.

The figure of Mary has been studied extensively in various contexts in a number of popular studies. I will touch here on only few of the lesser known but significant threads that are of particular practical use in Magical Christianity.

Even today, most people picture Mary as mild and meek—at best, an unsuspecting pawn in a great cosmic plan. Yet in popular medieval lore, she was anything but sweet, weak, or unaware. John of Garland (active ca. 1205–1255) in his *Stella Maris*[14] brings much of this lore together, for example, presenting Mary as the entire night sky, in other words, as the universal sky goddess. Taking over a classical image, Garland has the Milky Way formed of milk spurted from her breast.

But Garland's work is also influenced by less literary sources, such as the little-known Elements Cycle, a widely popular group of medieval tales about Mary's power over water, earth, air, and fire.[15] Though the style of the stories is often profane, the Elements Cycle has a deep underlying metaphysics, namely, that Mary is the supreme initiatrix of the four elements, the goddess of earth and matter, and mother of creation.

Mary also has a curious connection to the ancient protective amulet (still popular in Judaism today) known as the Hand of Miryam. The Hand of Miryam has the form of a three-fingered hand with a curved thumb—like a crescent moon or sickle—on either side. (Often there is an eye or a spiral on the palm.) Interestingly, this image first appears on monuments to the goddess Tanit, a Phoenician variant of Anat, whom we met earlier in this chapter.

In Islam the same amulet is known as the Hand of Fatima, referring to Mohammed's daughter Fatima Zahra. In Islamic esoteric (Sufi)
tradition, Fatima is considered to have been the spiritual "pole" or Axis
of her time. She is also known as "the greater Mary," in reference to the
spiritual lineage of Mary of Nazareth (that is, the Myriam tradition).

This strange magical image of the Hand of the Goddess, then,
runs through the three great Western religions and links them to their
roots in the power of the divine feminine.

THE "THREE SISTERHOODS"

Although I have listed out the nine New Testament Marys individually, they can also be grouped in several other ways, the most common
being seven or three. Rather than take these views as mutually exclusive, however, it is far more helpful from a practical esoteric stand-
point to see three complementary sisterhoods. The Three Sisterhoods,
composed of nine, seven, and three Marys respectively (table 3), are
derived from the way the Mary figures have merged into one another
in various legends, tales, texts, and commentaries.

Table 3. *The figures of Mary and the "Three Sisterhoods"*

NINE MARYS *Sisters of the Tree*	SEVEN MARYS *Sisters of the Veil*	THREE MARYS *Sisters of the Realms*
Mary of Nazareth (9)	Mary of Nazareth	Mary of Nazareth
Mary Jacobe (5)		*Celestial Realm*
The Other Mary (4)	Mary Jacobe	
Mary Cleopas (3)		
Mary of Rome (1)	Mary of Rome	
Mary Salome (8)	Mary Salome	Mary Salome
		Terrestrial Realm
Mary of Magdala (7)	Mary of Magdala	Mary of Magdala
Mary of Bethany (4)	Mary of Bethany	*UnderRealm*
Mary the Hostess (2)	Mary the Hostess	
and Miryam the Prophetess		

The Nine Miryams or Marys, together with Miryam the Prophetess, constitute a fairly comprehensive inner lineage that fits well with the pattern of the Qabalistic Tree (figure 16). They could thus be called the Sisters of the Tree. For those who know how to use it, the Tree provides a well-structured method for working in vision and ritual that can open up powerful realizations and resonances.

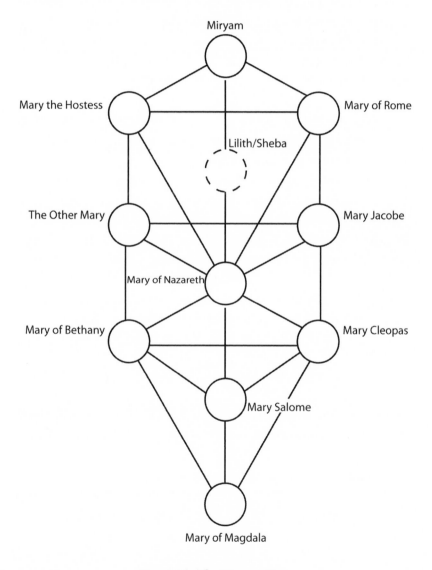

Figure 16. *The Miryam Tree*

The pattern of seven Marys links to legendary tales of a sisterhood of virgins who wove the veil before the Holy of Holies. According to the Protevangelion of James, seven virgins were chosen to weave the veil of the Temple, among them Mary of Nazareth, who wove the purple thread of royalty. The legend was popular in Eastern Orthodox tradition, appearing in a Byzantine mosaic in the Chora Church in Turkey. (Interestingly, Chora means "container" and refers to Mary as *hē Chōra tou Achōrētou* or "Container of the Uncontainable.")

Several Eastern European folk traditions seem to draw upon this legend. For instance, to protect a village from plague, seven girls named Mary must weave a veil, which is then hung on a tree outside the village.

The powers of the Seven are those of revealing and concealing, and, among other things, the Sisters of the Veil can be invoked in the seven directions as a means of protection.

The Three Marys can be called upon when a quantity of focused power is needed, especially in a ritual context. The Three Marys might be called the Sisters of the Realms, because they are connected to the Three Realms as follows: Mary of Nazareth, to the Celestial Realm (including the planets and the Moon); Mary of Magdala, to the UnderRealm (the realm of ancestors and bloodlines); Mary Salome, to the Terrestrial Realm (as midwife and dancer, she is a giver and taker of life and thus occupies the mortal realm of birth and death).

The Marys and the Grail

Finally, we note that the Three Marys can each be associated with a particular aspect of the Grail:

- Mary of Nazareth bears the Child of Light.
- Mary of Magdala bears the bloodline (SangReal).
- Mary Salome bears the prophesying, severed head of John the Baptist.

In Magical Christianity, the Grail functions in its various manifestations as the vessel of grace. Indeed it seems likely that the word "grail" ultimately derives from *gratialis*—a Latin compound of the feminine noun *gratia* (grace) and the ending *alis*. *Gratialis* thus translates as "vessel of grace."[16]

This connection is interesting because from an esoteric Christian perspective, grace (*charis*) is the power of the Holy Spirit that enables magical abilities, including prophecy, which as we have seen has a special connection to the Miryam tradition.

Now, prophetic power does not necessarily generate apocalyptic visions; rather, it can be quite individualized and personal. How it expresses itself depends to some degree on spiritual function and personal need at a particular moment. We conclude this chapter and this book with an invitation to explore this and other issues related to the Miryam tradition in the exercise below.

V I S I O N   E X E R C I S E

The Hand of Miryam

The following vision departs from the previous exercises in this book both in style of practice and in depth of content.

It should be considered a launching pad for further work with the Miryam tradition. The exercise draws together a number of important threads we have considered in this chapter and opens up several more. Note that this vision is not included on the CD accompanying this book.

L ight a candle and see its smoke become a pillar of cloud. Step in vision through the cloud.

You are on the shore of an inland sea. A woman is walking toward you over the water, her long red hair rising and falling on the waves about her. She starts to dance on the water and as she does so the sea turns to blood, the blood of her ancestors and her descendents, the blood of the line of Miryam.

She dances across the sea to the shore where you stand. She spins her blood-soaked hair, spattering your body and face, blinding you with crimson—thick and wet. You wipe your eyes, looking though the haze of blood, and see her still dancing. Her whirling hair, now dried, picks up a cloud of dust and dirt. The cloud spins close, and you find yourself drawn into its dark turning.

You are in the whirlwind, pushing forward through the biting dust until you break into stillness. There in the eye of the cyclone burn seven lamps before seven sisters kneeling in a circle around the Miryam. They face out from the center and their long hair weaves together across the ground, becoming the Miryam's hair. She is covered entirely by her hair, which hangs about her like a red cloak.

The nearest women pierce you with stark looks as you walk into the circle and kneel before the Miryam. She parts the thickness of her hair, revealing her radiant torso and the sacred image known as the Hand of Miryam tattooed on her belly. The hand has three fingers and two thumbs, which curve on either side of the palm like waxing and waning crescent moons. The lines on the palm spiral around a central eye.

You look at your own hands. Then, laying the palm of one against the back of the other, you touch her tattoo, which shimmers like moonlight. You are drawn into her belly, into the stillness and utter darkness of the Void.

A mighty hand presses out of that darkness, as if to push you away. But you reach forward and gently lay your own palm against it.

The hand becomes the hand of a small child. And that hand draws you in, into a place of power, of protection, of vision, expression, and utterance. You feel the power of the Child running into you through your hand, and you allow yourself to be given over to that power as it stirs the gift of prophecy within you . . .

(pause as needed)

When you are finished, the Child's hand slips out of yours. Fire rises about you as you step forward and emerge from the flame of your candle and return to your place within the room. When you are ready, open your eyes, extinguish the flame and write down your experience.

APPENDIX: KENOSIS

CD Track 1

enosis comes from the Greek *kenos*, "empty," with reference to the tradition that the Logos "emptied itself" in order to incarnate (cf. Phil. 2:7). Thus the exercise below should be undertaken in an attitude of contemplation. Ideally, one empties oneself of all imbalance and distraction, that one may be filled with the divine presence.

You are sitting comfortably, back straight, feet flat on the floor, your palms resting upon your thighs. Begin with controlled, regular breathing (four counts per in-breath and four counts per out-breath). Be aware of the rhythmic attunement of your entire being to your breath, and recall that the breath symbolizes the movement of the Spirit.

Now consciously allow deep peace and stillness to penetrate the levels of your being one at a time. Still your physical body first: Your tensions dissipate, your muscles relax, your heartbeat slows, and all the internal processes of your body function in quiescent harmony. Now still your desires and emotions, allowing them to become harmonized, to be absorbed into the great flow of Being. Let your thoughts too become still. Concentrate only upon your breathing. Empty yourself of all else. There is only the breathing, the rhythm of the Deep Peace.

ℋOTES

INTRODUCTION

1. This rather eloquent term, "Son of Light," referring to the living Logos, is found in the Aramaic traditions of the Magi, in the Coptic Gnostic texts of the Nag Hammadi Library, and in certain Celtic traditions of Scotland and northern England.

2. Ultimately, all of the cosmos, inward and outward, is potentially symbolic. It is a matter of discovering or learning to read what the ancients called "the book of nature" that is at issue.

3. It is not for nothing that Christ appears as the Gardener to Mary Magdelene (John 20:15), nor is it without import that he is called "the True Vine" and "the Tree of Life." And there is profound significance in the use of the word "neophyte" (literally, "new plant") to describe one newly entered in the mysteries.

CHAPTER 1

1. Arnet Jan Wensinck, "The Ideas of the Western Semites Concerning the Navel of the Earth," *Verhandelingen der Koninklijke Akademie van Westenschappen*, 2nd series, 17, no. 1 (1917).

2. As with all primordial symbols, the cosmic egg or sphere, or both, is found in sacred contexts (myths, rituals, legends, songs, etc.) throughout the world. One finds the image in areas as diverse and far-flung as Polynesia, Indonesia, Estonia, Latvia, Finland, Persia, Peru, Central America, West Africa, Egypt, Japan, China, Tibet, India, Arabia, and others. See Anna-Britta Hellbom, "The Creation Egg," *Ethnos* 1 (1963).

3. The recurrence in the Christian tradition of these two images, either singly or together, was undoubtedly aided and abetted by the influence of the Neoplatonist philosophers, whose powerful impact on Christian mystical philosophy and metaphysics is undisputed: "Let us then form a mental image of this cosmos . . . so that whatever . . . comes first into the mind as the 'one' (as for instance, the outermost sphere of the fixed stars), there immediately follows also the sight of the semblance of the sun, and together with it that of the other stars or planetary spheres, and the earth and sea, and all things living, as though in one transparent sphere. . . . Let there then be in the soul some semblance of a sphere of light, having all things in it. . . . Then invoking God who has made the reality of which you hold the phantom in your consciousness, pray that He may come." Plotinus (ca. AD 250), quoted in G. R. S. Mead, *Quests, Old and New* (London: G. Bell & Sons, Ltd., 1913). And according to Macrobius (ca. AD 410), the egg was greatly revered in the mysteries "because of its oval, almost spherical, shape which has no opening of any kind, and because it contains life in itself." Louis Charbonneau-Lassay, *The Bestiary of Christ* (New York: Arkana, 1992).

4. Alexander Roberts and James Donaldson, eds., *The Ante-Nicene Fathers*, vol. 8 (Edinburgh: T. and T. Clark, 1868).

5. J. P. Migne, *Patrologia cursus completus Latina*, vol. 172 (Paris: Garnier Fratres, 1844).

6. Ibid., vol. 197.

7. Julian of Norwich, *Showings* (New York: Paulist Press, 1978).

8. M. T. d'Alverny, *Alain de Lille: Textes Inedits* (Paris: J. Urin, 1965).

9. "Now for that Living Creature which is designed to embrace within itself all living creatures the fitting shape will be that which comprises within itself all the shapes there are; wherefore He wrought it into a round, in the shape of a sphere. . . ." Plato, *Timaeus* 33.

10. This concept is easier to visualize in two-dimensional terms. For example, the area of a circle of a given circumference is greater than the area of, say, a square with the same perimeter.

11. For a more detailed consideration of the Three Regions, see chapters 6 and 7.

12. Hartley Burr Alexander, *Mythology of All Races*, vol. 10: North American (New York: Cooper Square Publishers, 1964).

13. Nigel Pennick, *The Ancient Science of Geomancy* (London: Thames and Hudson, 1979).

14. Witness the medieval practice of reciting the creation text of Genesis 1 during the Easter Vigil. Closely related also are certain astrological factors that link Easter and the creation myth. The sun, along with the moon in its full phase, was created at the beginning of time, that is, in Aries, the first sign of the Zodiac. Likewise, Easter is traditionally dated each year with reference to the first full moon occurring after the sun has entered the sign Aries (the spring equinox).

15. "But when a new people was created . . . , it was no longer necessary for them to observe the end of the first creation, but rather to seek the beginning of the second. And what is this, but the day on which the Lord rose again. It is from here that the new creation began. . . . God ceased His making of the first creation . . . ; but the second creation has no end." Athanasius, *de sabbatis*. Quoted in Jean Danielou, *The Bible and the Liturgy* (Notre Dame, IN: University of Notre Dame, 1956).

16. J. A. MacCulloch, *The Harrowing of Hell* (London: Clark, 1930).

17. Venetia Newall, "Easter Eggs," *Folklore* 79 (Winter 1968).

18. Charbonneau-Lassay, *The Bestiary of Christ*.

19. Newall, "Easter Eggs."

20. Mircea Eliade, *Patterns in Comparative Religion* (New York: Meridian, 1958).

21. Interesting too is that the rendering of the *vesica piscis* or mandorla is related to the "squaring of the circle," which itself lies at the root of certain esoteric Masonic traditions incorporated into the cathedrals of the Middle Ages. In a certain sense, the square (or cube) represents the manifestation or fulfillment of the potentiality inherent in the circle (or sphere) Thus the sphere of creation becomes ultimately the foursquare "New Jerusalem," the restoration of the paradisal realm on a new level.

22. Certain legends speak of Adam as originally having a spherical body.

CHAPTER 2

1. Mircea Eliade, *Shamanism* (New York: Bollingen, 1964).

2. J. P. Migne, *Patrologia cursus completus Graeca*, vol. 11 (Paris: Garnier Fratres, 1857).

3. Another important image that developed out of the ladder (and which serves a similar function) is the mystic spiral stair.

4. Edward C. Sellner, *Wisdom of the Celtic Saints* (Notre Dame, IN: Ave Maria, 1993).

5. J. P. Migne, *Patrologia cursus completus Latina*, vol. 173 (Paris: Garnier Fratres, 1844).

6. Charles Coüasnon, *The Church of the Holy Sepulchre in Jerusalem* (London: Oxford University Press, 1974).

7. J. P. Migne, *Patrologia cursus completus Graeca*, vol. 92 (Paris: Garnier Fratres, 1857).

8. Ibid., vol. 132.

9. Eliade, *Patterns in Comparative Religion*.

10. Woodcut reproduced in Frederick William Hackwood, *Christ Lore: Being the Legends, Traditions, Myths, Symbols, Customs, and Superstitions of the Christian Church* (London: Elliot Stock, 1902).

11. The three types of tree usually mentioned are the palm, the cypress, and the cedar. These three have had their own folklore and symbolism for millennia. The symbolism marks each tree as pertaining, among other things, to one of the Three Cosmic Regions. The attributions are briefly as follows:

    - The palm is associated with eternity, purity, and the Celestial Realm.
    - The cypress is linked with the rites of death and mourning and relates to the UnderRealm.
    - The cedar is as associated particularly with regeneration and cyclic processes. It is thus attributed to the Middle Region or Terrestrial Realm.

- The fusion of the trees reflects the power of the staff over the forces of the Three Realms, and also the power of the Cross as the instrument of regeneration and redemption of the whole cosmos.

12. The mention of the wood of the Cross as a structural component of the original Temple connects to a stream of esoteric teaching regarding the relationship of the body of Christ to the sacred edifice. In the legend, the proto-cross that will bear the body of Christ becomes the door leading to the divine presence. The traditions encapsulated here find their way well into the Middle Ages and reach their flowering in the Gothic period. The form of the church was based upon both the mystical body of Christ and the Cosmic Cross, which were symbolically fused at the Crucifixion.

13. George Every, *Christian Mythology* (Feltham, England: Hamlyn, 1970).

14. The loss of memory of primordial matters is a notion common to many esoteric traditions. In spiritual terms, human beings are seen as falling away from a primal state of perfection. The idea is at the root of those ritual patterns and practices which themselves reflect or embody temporal and cyclic structures, as well as those which are fitted to a "calendar," as in the calendar of saints. The practical significance of these cyclical or spiral patterns is that they enable the recreation of a primordial event on a recurring (usually yearly) cycle. One might say that linear time is in this way altered to a sacred pattern. Spiritual forces are enabled to spill into the flow of time, saturating the present with primordial power, thus in a sense redeeming time. There are deep and important reasons for the early Christian references to Christ as the *anniculus*, the "One Year Old." Joseph Gaer, *The Lore of the New Testament* (Boston: Little, Brown, 1952).

15. This doctrine is rather more fully developed in a cycle of traditional stories about the Magi. The Chronicle of Zuquin, for instance, relates how the Magi climb the World Mountain every year to look for signs of the coming redeemer. Eventually a star appears and a divine child descends in a pillar of light to tell the Magi to go to Bethlehem, As the Magi near the cave where the Redeemer is being born, they see a pillar of light descend to the cave, filling it with a light brighter than the sun.

16. J. P. Migne, *Patrologia cursus completus Graeca*, vol. 94 (Paris: Garnier Fratres, 1857).

17. John Henry Grafton Grattan and Charles Joseph Singer, *Anglo-Saxon Magic and Medicine* (London: Oxford University Press, 1952).

18. Teresa of Avila, *The Collected Works of St. Teresa of Avila* (Washington, DC: Institute of Carmelite Studies, 1976).

19. Jean Danielou, *Primitive Christian Symbols* (Baltimore: Helicon Press, 1964).

20. Sabine Baring-Gould, *Curious Myths of the Middle Ages* (London: Rivington's, 1868). See also Alban Butler, *Butler's Lives of the Saints*, ed. Herbert Thurston and Donald Attwater (New York: Kennedy, 1956).

21. J. G. Davies, *The Architectural Setting of Baptism* (London: Barrie and Rockliff, 1962).

22. Was it not thou
    that didst cut Rahab in pieces,
    that didst pierce the dragon?
    Was it not thou that didst dry up the Sea,
    the waters of the great deep. . . ? (Isa. 51:9–10)

    Note also that the myth of the primordial dragon-slaying is here linked to the separation of the waters of Genesis 1.

23. Probably the charge laid by the Inquisition that the Knights Templar worshipped a head has its basis in secret teachings of the order regarding Christ as the Cosmic Center. This interpretation would tie in with traditions regarding the Holy Sepulcher, Golgotha, and the Head of Adam said to have been buried at the foot of the Cross.

CHAPTER 3

1. David Walsh, *The Mysticism of Innerworldly Fulfillment* (Gainesville: University of Florida, 1983).

2. Jonathan Barnes, *Early Greek Philosophy* (New York: Penguin, 1987).

3. R. J. Stewart, *The Elements of Creation Myth* (Shaftsbury, Dorset: Element, 1989).

4. Mircea Eliade, *History of Religious Ideas* (Chicago: University of Chicago Press, 1978).

5. The Bhagavad-Gita, trans. Georg Feuerstein (New Delhi: Arnold-Heinemann, 1981).

6. Mircea Eliade, *The Two and the One* (New York: Sheed and Ward, 1965).

7. Ibid.

8. *The Secret Teachings of Jesus*, trans. Marvin Meyer (New: York, Random House, 1984)

9. Marco Polo, *The Description of the World*, trans. A. C. Moule and Paul Pelliot (London: Routledge & Sons, 1938). See also Jacques Duchesne-Guillemin, *Symbols and Values in Zoroastrianism* (New York: Harper and Row, 1966).

10. Richard Rolle, *The Fire of Love*, trans. Clifton Wolters (New York: Penguin, 1972).

11. Joseph Stierli, ed. *Heart of the Savior* (New York: Herder, 1958).

12. Carl-Martin Edsman, "Fire," *The Encyclopedia of Religion*. ed. Mircea Eliade. 15 vols. (New York: Macmillan, 1987). See also R. H. Charles, ed., *Apocrypha and Pseudepigrapha of the Old Testament in English: With Introductions and Critical and Explanatory Notes to the Several Books*. 2 vols. (Oxford: Clarendon Press, 1913).

13. In a related legend, it is John standing nearby who catches the blood that runs after Thomas's touch and soaks it into some bread kept over from the Last Supper. This was kept as a healing unction and used to bless the Host.

14. J. P. Migne, *Patrologia cursus completus Graeca*, vol. 65 (Paris: Garnier Fratres, 1857).

15. Ibid.

16. Alan Watts, *Myth and Ritual in Christianity* (Boston: Beacon Press, 1968).

17. Carl-Martin Edsman, *Le Baptême de Feu* (Uppsala: Almquist & Wiksells, 1940).

18. Anan Isho, *The Paradise or Garden of the Holy Fathers*, trans. E. A. Wallis Budge (New York: Duffield & Company, 1909).

19. David Marshall Lang, *Lives and Legends of the Georgian Saints* (New York: St. Vladimir's, 1956).

20. See Acts 17:32 after Paul's talk on the Unknown God.

21. Otto Georg von Simson, *The Gothic Cathedral* (New York: Pantheon Books, 1956).

22. Dionysius the Areopagite, *The Complete Works* (New York: Paulist Press, 1987).

23. Ibid.

24. Edsman, *Le Baptême de Feu*.

25. Ibid.

26. The use of white robes specifically reflects the initiate's spiritual participation in the mystery of the Transfiguration: "And His face shone like the sun, and His garments became as white as light" (Matt. 17:2). In the realm of symbolic structures, light and fire are often synonymous images.

27. Liturgically, the relationship between the two elements is epitomized in the ritual mixing of the water and wine (liquid fire), which is itself linked both to the flow of water and blood from Christ's side at the Crucifixion and to Christ's changing of water into wine at Cana. The latter episode, significantly, is celebrated at the Feast of the Epiphany—along with Easter and Pentecost, one of the three days traditionally set aside for the initiation rites.

28. John Climacus, *The Ladder of Divine Ascent*, trans. Archimandrite Lazarus Moore (London: Faber and Faber, 1959).

29. Carl-Martin Edsman, "Fire," in *The Encyclopedia of Religion*, ed. Mircea Eliade (New York: Macmillan, 1987).

30. Edsman, *Le Bapteme de Feu*.

31. Dionysius the Areopagite, *The Complete Works*.

32. Charles, *Apocrypha and Pseudepigrapha*. See also Edsman, *Le Baptême de Feu*.

33. The tradition is given from a slightly different angle in *The Chronicon Pascal*, which remarks how, when Jesus came out of the water at the Baptism, "The heavens were straight away opened and the Holy Ghost came in the shape of a dove resembling fire. . . ." See Edsman, *Le Bapteme de Feu*.

34. Danielou, *The Bible and the Liturgy*. See also Migne, *Patrologia cursus completus Graeca*, vol. 11.

35. Dionysius the Areopagite, *The Complete Works*.

36. F. Ohrt, "The Spark in the Water," *FF Communications* 65 (1926).

37. Ibid.

38. This is, however, rarely the glamorous work it is sometimes thought to be. Archetypal patterns are usually worked out in the apparently quite unexciting daily life of the initiate. Mediation often takes place unseen, without fanfare, praise, acknowledgment, or understanding from those around one.

CHAPTER 4

1. Francois Pettipierre, "The Symbolic Landscape of the Muiscas," *Studies in Comparative Religion*, Winter (1979): 36–51.

2. Alfonso Ortiz, *The Tewa World* (Chicago: University of Chicago Press, 1969).

3. W. R. Lethaby, *Architecture, Mysticism and Myth* (London: The Architectural Press, 1891).

4. John Kirtland Wright, *The Geographical Lore of the Time of the Crusades* (New York: American Geographical Society, 1925).

5. Ibid.

6. Ibid.

7. Dante Alighieri, *The Divine Comedy*, trans. Dorothy L. Sayers (Baltimore: Penguin, 1949).

8. Robert L. Cohn, *The Shape of Sacred Space* (Chico, CA: Scholars Press, 1981).

9. Ibid.

10. According to Plato, Apollo is the god who "sits upon the stone at the center of the earth." (*Republic* 427b).

11. Lethaby, *Architecture, Mysticism and Myth*.

12. E. Baldwin Smith, *The Dome* (Princeton: Princeton, NJ: University Press, 1956).

13. Zev Vilnay, *Legends of Jerusalem* (Philadelphia: Jewish Publication Society of America, 1973).

14. Titus Burckhardt, *Art of Islam: Language and Meaning* (London: World of Islam Festival Pub. Co, 1976).

15. Johnathan Z. Smith, "Earth and Gods." *The Journal of Religion* 49, No. 2, (1969): 103–128.

16. Ibid.

17. Luke Timothy Johnson, *The Writings of the New Testament* (Philadelphia: Fortress Press, 1986).

18. Mircea Eliade, *The Sacred and the Profane* (New York: Harcourt, Brace & World, 1959).

19. E. D. Hunt, *Holy Land Pilgrimage in the Later Roman Empire AD 312–460* (Oxford: Clarendon Press, 1982).

20. Such experiences always involve a certain merging of planes and by nature present peculiar difficulties for expression and understanding. It is an all too common occurrence, even among trained esotericists, for an experience of a fusion of the planes to lead to one's permanently confusing the planes. Thus, the ability to discern among spiritual things is traditionally ranked as one of the more important qualities an initiate should cultivate. Whether Nicholas and Melito both erred in taking a spiritual vision for a physical one, however, is unclear for several reasons, not the least of which is the simple fact that they lived in a milieu where the planes were closer together than is the case in our modern era.

21. Coüasnon, *The Church of the Holy Sepulchre in Jerusalem*.

22. Ephraem Syrus, *The Book of the Cave of Treasures*, trans. E. A. Wallis

Budge (London: Religious Tract Society, 1927).

23. Eliade, *Patterns in Comparative Religion.*

24. Hunt, *Holy Land Pilgrimage in the Later Roman Empire AD 312–460.*

25. Charles, *Apocrypha and Pseudepigrapha.*

26. Roberts and Donaldson, *The Ante-Nicene Fathers*, vol. 8, Clement of Rome, homily 17. See also Alan Watts, *Myth and Ritual in Christianity* (Boston: Beacon Press, 1968).

27. Charles, *Apocrypha and Pseudepigrapha.*

28. Davies, *The Architectural Setting of Baptism.*

29. Ibid.

30. Charles, *Apocrypha and Pseudepigrapha.*

31. Most notably, Christ's Descent to the UnderRealm and the story of Seth's search for the oil of mercy.

32. Emma Jung and Marie-Louise von Franz, *The Grail Legend*, trans. Andrea Dykes (London: Conventure, 1970). Also A. Pauphilet, ed., *La Quest du Saint Graal*, Paris: Champion, 1923).

33. Ibid.

34. We find the same esoteric symbolism in a work of Honorius of Autun on the liturgy. He writes, "When the priest says *per omnia saecula saeculorum*, the deacon comes before him and elevates the chalice. He covers a portion of it with a cloth, then returns it to the altar and covers it with the corporal, enacting the part of Joseph of Arimethea who took the body of Christ down from the cross, covered his face with a sudarium, laid the body in the grave and covered it with a stone. That which is here offered, and also the chalice, are covered with the corporeal, which signifies the linen winding sheet in which Joseph wrapped the body of Christ. The Chalice signifies the grave, and the paten the stone with which it was closed" (quoted in Jung and von Franz, *The Grail Legend*). The symbolism goes back much further than this, however, at least to fourth-century Syria. The *Homilies* of Theodore of Mopsuestia say that "it is in a

sort of tomb that Christ is placed on the altar. That is why some of the deacons, who lay out the cloths on the altar, show by this action the likeness of the burial cloths." See Danielou, *The Bible and the Liturgy.*

35. Lethaby, *Architecture, Mysticism and Myth.*

36. von Simson, *The Gothic Cathedral.*

37. Ibid.

38. Maximus the Confessor, *Selected Writings*, trans. George Berthold (New York: Paulist Press, 1985).

CHAPTER 5

1. J. P. Migne, *Patrologia cursus completus Latina*, vol. 4 (Paris: Garnier Fratres, 1844).

2. Because of his vehement polemic towards certain "Gnostic" sects, Irenaeus is generally dismissed as a despiser of all things esoteric. This view, however, is inaccurate. Irenaeus's truculence stems not from his dislike of esoteric tradition, but from his desire to protect or preserve what he considered the true esoteric teachings from corruption by certain creation-negating influences current within some of the Gnostic systems of the second century. Read with discretion, Ireneaus's works yield many gems of esoteric wisdom.

3. J. P. Migne, *Patrologia cursus completus Graeca*, vol. 8 (Paris: Garnier Fratres, 1857).

4. Which, as he remarks, derive from Ezekiel's vision of the Tetramorphs (Ez. 10:14).

5. Raphael in the Book of Tobit; Gabriel in Daniel and Luke; Michael in Daniel, Jude, and Revelation; Uriel in 2 Esdras.

6. Migne, *Patrologia cursus completus Graeca*, vol. 11. See also Danielou, *Primitive Christian Symbols.*

7. Ireneaus. "Epideixis," in J. A. Robinson, trans., *The Demonstration of the Apostolic Preaching* (London: Society For Promoting Christian Knowledge, 1920), I, 34.

8. At one time, the Epiphany was likely celebrated on the first new moon after the winter solstice.

9. Danielou, *The Bible and the Liturgy.*

10. Ibid.

11. Saint Gregory Palamas, *The Triads*, trans. John Meyendorff (New York: Paulist Press, 1983).

12. Ibid.

13. Maximus the Confessor, *Selected Writings.*

14. Marvin Meyer, trans., *The Secret Teachings of Jesus* (New York: Random House, 1984), Logion 75.

15. The Descent, though not specifically mentioned in the conventional Gospels, is at least alluded to in Matthew 13, and it has an important place in many apocryphal works, the most important being the Gospel of Nicodemus.

16. MacCulloch, *The Harrowing of Hell.*

17. Danielou, *The Bible and the Liturgy.*

18. Cited in MacCulloch, *The Harrowing of Hell.*

19. Ibid.

20. Montague Rhodes James, *The Apocryphal New Testament: Being the Apocryphal Gospels, Acts, Epistles, and Apocalypses, with Other Narratives and Fragments* (Oxford: Clarendon Press, 1924).

21. The actual date of the entry of the sun into each sign varies slightly from year to year. Those with astrological knowledge can work out the exact dates for themselves.

22. According to the Acts of John, the Logos is "the harmony of wisdom" and "wisdom in harmony." And in the Acts of Peter: "What else is Christ but the sound (i.e., harmony) of God."

23. "In the beginning was the Logos,
    and the Logos was with God,
    and the Logos was God.
    It was in the beginning with God.

All things came into being by It,
and apart from It nothing came into being
that has come into being." (John 1:1–3)

Chapter 6

1. According to Eusebius, who speaks of the "three sacred places revered for three mystical caves," the Ascension took place from a cave in the Mount of Olives. Hunt, *Holy Land Pilgrimage*.

2. The word "Eve" literally means "Life."

3. Dante Alighieri, *The Divine Comedy*, trans. Dorothy L. Sayers. (Baltimore: Penguin, 1949).

4. Remember, all of the souls in Dante's *Inferno* are there because they ultimately refuse to change for the better.

5. Baring-Gould, *Curious Myths of the Middle Ages*.

6. J. P. Migne, *Patrologia cursus completus Graeca*, vol. 7 (Paris: Garnier Fratres, 1857). See also Jean Danielou, "Traditions Secretes des Apôtres," *Eranos-Jahrbuch* 32 (1962): 199–215.

7. Migne, *Patrologia cursus completus Graeca*, vol. 8; also Danielou, "Traditions Secretes des Apôtres."

Chapter 7

1. *Ordo rerum talis esse invenitur, ut ab uno extremo ad alterum non pervenientur nisi per media.*

2. Each plane "enables" and transforms the planes below it.

3. This is one facet of the role and value of the mystery schools, which provide time-tested methodology, philosophy, and ethics for dealing with the energies and entities of the inner planes.

4. For more details on the three orders of contact, see my small book *Contacting Spiritual Beings* (Oceanside, CA: Sun Chalice Books, 2002).

5. And, if in a ritual context, simultaneously arranged or presented on the external plane.

6. Peter Brown, *The Cult of the Saints* (Chicago: Universtity of Chicago Press, 1981).

7. This is the origin of the adoption of Christian names. The taking on of the name of a saint was part of a process of bringing the soul under the protection and guidance of that saint.

8. Brown, *The Cult of the Saints.*

9. Ibid.

10. Dionysius the Areopagite, *The Complete Works.* It might be useful to recall that the word "perfection" means simply "to be made whole."

11. Ibid.

12. Eliade, *History of Religious Ideas.*

13. Gregory Palamas, *The Triads*, trans. John Meyendorff (New York: Paulist Press, 1983).

14. Ibid.

CHAPTER 8

1. Mary is the anglicized form of *Maria*, which is the Greek form of the Hebrew *Miryam*.

2. Karel van der Toorn, "Anat-Yahu, Some Other Deities, and the Jews of Elephantine," *Numen* 39, No. 1 (1992): 80–101.

3. Eliade, *History of Religious Ideas.*

4. Raphael Patai, *The Hebrew Goddess*, 3d ed. (Detroit: Wayne State University Press, 1990).

5. In the myth, Anat winnows Mot, the god of Death and the Under-Realm.

6. Eliade, *History of Religious Ideas.*

7. This same power also influences the theological speculations of Dionysius the Areopagite, the anonymous author of *The Cloud of Unknowing*, and Meister Eckhart and is reflected in the popular adoration of the Black Madonnas.

8. Her rebel nature brings to mind the legends of Lilith, Adam's first wife and a major figure in the feminine mysteries of magical Christianity.

9. In early alchemical works Miryam is also identified with Maria Prophetissa, who was the first to find the Philosopher's Stone.

10. J. Frank Henderson, "Where Have All the Marys Gone?" *National Bulletin on Liturgy* 28, no. 141 (1995): 122–126.

11. Benjamin Walker, *Gnosticism: Its History and Influence* (Wellingsborough, UK: The Aquarian Press, 1983).

12. The apocryphal Gospel of Bartholomew also mentions "Salome who tempted him" (i.e., Jesus). See James, *The Apocryphal New Testament.*

13. Ibid.

14. Evelyn Faye Wilson, *The Stella Maris of John of Garland; Edited, Together with a Study of Certain Collections of Mary Legends Made in Northern France in the Twelfth and Thirteenth Centuries* (Cambridge, MA: Mediaeval Academy of America, 1946).

15. Ibid.

16. Most scholars agree that the word Grail, and its variants Graal and Gral, derives from the Latin word *gradalis*. However, there is considerable difference of opinion when it comes to the origins of that word itself. Some hold that *gradalis* comes from *gradualis*—in English, a gradual—a book containing the choral parts of the Mass. Others suggest that it derives from a compound of the Greek word *krater* (a large drinking vessel) and the suffix *alis* which is used in medieval Latin to describe a container or vessel of some sort. See Henry and Renée Kahane, *The Krater and the Grail* (Urbana: University of Illinois Press, 1965). I believe I am the first to suggest that *gradalis* is a corruption of *gratialis*, "vessel of grace."

$\mathcal{S}$ELECTED $\mathcal{B}$IBLIOGRAPHY

AUTHOR'S NOTE: *Although this is not an academic work, the nature of our subject has required the consultation of more than one obscure academic tome and, in some cases, even the translation (or retranslation) of relevant traditions from original sources. All sources are cited in the endnotes. The following bibliography has been limited to more readily available or accessible texts. Of these, titles marked with an asterisk (*) are of special importance.*

Alighieri, Dante. *The Divine Comedy*. Translated by Dorothy L. Sayers. Baltimore: Penguin, 1949.*

Baring-Gould, Sabine. *Curious Myths of the Middle Ages*. London: Rivington's, 1868.*

Brown, Coleston. *Contacting Spiritual Beings*. Oceanside, CA: Sun Chalice, 2002.*

Butler, Alban. *Butler's Lives of the Saints*. Edited by Herbert Thurston and Donald Attwater. New York: Kennedy, 1956.

Campbell, Joseph, ed. *The Mysteries*. New York: Bollingen, 1955.

Charbonneau-Lassay, Louis. *The Bestiary of Christ*. New York: Arkana, 1992.*

Charles, R. H., ed. *Apocrypha and Pseudepigrapha of the Old Testament in English: With Introductions and Critical and Explanatory Notes to the Several Books*. 2 vols. (Oxford: Clarendon Press, 1913).

Cloud of Unknowing, The. New York: Paulist Press, 1981.*

Dionysius the Areopagite. *The Complete Works*. New York: Paulist Press, 1987.*

Duncan, Anthony. *The Lord of the Dance*. Oceanside, CA: Sun Chalice Books, 1996.*

Edsman, Carl-Martin. "Fire." In *The Encyclopedia of Religion*, edited by Mircea Eliade. New York: Macmillan, 1987.

Eliade, Mircea. *History of Religious Ideas*. Chicago: University of Chicago Press, 1978.

———. *Patterns in Comparative Religion*. New York: Meridian, 1958.

Every, George. *Christian Mythology*. Feltham: Hamlyn, 1970.

Fideler, David. *Jesus Christ, Sun of God*. Wheaton, IL: Theosophical Publishing House, Quest Books, 1993.

Gaer, Joseph. *The Lore of the New Testament*. Boston: Little, Brown, 1952.*

Gregory Palamas. *The Triads*. Translated by John Meyendorff. New York: Paulist Press, 1983.*

Guénon, René. *The Symbolism of the Cross*. London: Luzac, 1958.

Hilton, Walter. *The Ladder of Perfection*. Harmondsworth, UK: Penguin, 1957.

Hole, Christina. *Saints in Folklore*. London: Bell, 1966.

Houston, Siobhan. *Invoking Mary Magdalene: Accessing the Wisdom of the Divine Feminine*. Boulder, CO: Sounds True, 2006.

Jacobus de Voragine. *The Golden Legend*. Translated by Granger Ryan and Helmut Ripperger. New York: Longmans, Green and Co., 1941.

James, Montague Rhodes, trans., *The Apocryphal New Testament: Being the Apocryphal Gospels, Acts, Epistles, and Apocalypses, with Other Narratives and Fragments*. Oxford: Clarendeon Press, 1924.

Julian of Norwich. *Showings*. New York: Paulist Press, 1978.

Jung, Emma, and Marie-Louise von Franz. *The Grail Legend*. Translated by Andrea Dykes. London: Conventure, 1970.

Knight, Gareth. *A Practical Guide to Qabalistic Symbolism.* Cheltenham, UK: Helios, 1965. Reprint edition, New York: Samuel Weiser, 1978.

———. *Experience of the Inner Worlds.* Toddington, England: Helios, 1975. Reprint edition, New York: Samuel Weiser, 1993.*

———. *The Rose Cross and the Goddess.* Northhampshire, England: Aquarian, 1985. Revised edition published under the title *Evoking the Goddess,* Rochester, VT: Destiny Books, 1993.*

Maximus the Confessor. *Selected Writings.* New York: Paulist Press, 1985.

Meyer, Marvin, trans. *The Secret Teachings of Jesus.* New: York, Random House, 1984.

Pennick, Nigel. *The Ancient Science of Geomancy.* London: Thames and Hudson, 1979.

Polo, Marco. *The Description of the World.* Translated by A. C. Moule and Paul Pelliot. London: Routledge & Sons, 1938.

Roberts, Alexander, and James Donaldson, eds., *The Ante-Nicene Fathers,* vol. 8. Edinburgh: T. and T. Clark, 1868.

Rolle, Richard. *The Fire of Love.* Translated by Clifton Wolters. New York: Penguin, 1972.

Sellner, Edward C. *Wisdom of the Celtic Saints.* Notre Dame, IN: Ave Maria, 1993.

Simson, Otto Georg von. *The Gothic Cathedral.* New York: Pantheon Books, 1956.

Smoley, Richard. *Inner Christianity: A Guide to the Esoteric Tradition.* Boston, MA: Shambhala, 2002.

Stevenson, James. *The Catacombs: Life and Death in Early Christianity.* London: Thames and Hudson, 1978.

Vilnay, Zev. *Legends of Jerusalem.* Philadelphia: Jewish Publication Society of America, 1973.

Walsh, David. *The Mysticism of Innerworldly Fufillment.* Gainesville: University of Florida, 1983.

Watts, Alan. *Myth and Ritual in Christianity.* Boston: Beacon Press, 1968.

ℐNDEX

altar, 19, 25, 65–66, 102–3, 121, 127, 131, 157
androgyny, 21
angels, 10, 26, 42, 46–47, 77, 93, 117, 121
animals, 43, 45, 68, 73, 116–17
Apostles, 40, 58, 72, 73, 85–87, 90, 97, 99, 104, 135, 137
archangels, 73–74, 120–21
archetypes, 85, 87, 122
architecture, 17, 18, 55–56, 116
arrow, 31
autumn, 79, 93

baptism, 44–48, 63
Baptism of Christ, 81
baptism of fire, 45–48
Bartholomew, 47, 162
beatitudes, 124
Bethlehem, 17, 38, 127, 151
Bishop, 76
bleeding head, 33
burials, 17
burning bush, 8, 37

calendar, 76–79, 88, 90, 131, 151
catacombs, 14, 17, 98
cathedrals, 9, 18, 149
Cave of Ascension, 98
caves, 17, 33, 55, 61, 68, 98–99, 102, 160
Celestial Realm, 46, 76, 97–100, 105–7, 117, 138, 140, 150
Christ Child, 18, 38, 75, 80–81, 108
Christmas, 64, 80–81
Church Militant, 100
Church Triumphant, 100
Cloud of Unknowing, The, 43, 161
collective being, 81
communion, 121
compassion, 10
constellations, 10, 94, 108
contemplation, 92, 107, 109, 111, 122, 145

cornerstone, 11, 58
cosmogony, 15
cosmology, 33, 84
Creation, 15, 19, 22, 34, 50, 67, 91, 106, 107, 110, 131, 147, 152
creational energies, 82
Creator, 40
crosier, 25, 92
Cross, 15, 26–30, 34, 39, 46, 61–66, 75–76, 91, 126, 151–53
Crucifixion of Christ, 83
crypt, 18, 110, 137
crystals, 7, 35, 50–51, 94, 106, 110–11

dark cloud, 82, 122, 131
dawn, 22, 41–42, 71, 79, 92
deification, 82, 123
descent to the UnderRealm, 19
Dionysios the Areopagite, 43, 121
Divine Comedy (Dante), 56, 100, 155, 160
divinity, 71, 82–83
domes, 25
dove, 44, 51, 52, 81, 130, 155
dragon, 31–33, 45–46, 81, 108, 110, 152
dragon force, 46, 81
dusk, 71, 79
Dweller on the Threshold, 104, 119

eagle, 73, 75, 94
east, 57, 71, 73, 76, 80
Easter, 19, 80, 147, 152
Eden, 28, 29, 57
egg, 14–21, 135, 147, 148
elementals, 93, 117
enlightenment, 82, 83
entities, 10, 120, 160
Epiphany, 79, 154, 159
equinoxes, 78
etheric, 97
evocation, 124

Gabriel, 73, 74, 94, 158

Garden, 29, 57, 154
geometry, 15, 16, 20
gnosis, 85
gnostic, 39, 107
Goddess, 123, 130, 135, 136, 138, 161
goddesses, 117, 123, 130
gods, 85, 117, 123
Golgotha, 29, 59, 60, 63, 152
green, 6, 92, 94, 95, 109, 111
Guardians, 118

Hand of Miryam, The (exercise), 141
healer, 73, 85
heart, 30, 39, 40, 49, 52, 55, 58, 61, 69,
    125–27
hermit, 39–40
heroes, 117, 121
holy of holies, 57
Holy Sepulcher, 18, 59–64, 152

icons, 9, 20, 32
illumination, 8, 43–47, 51, 69, 75, 82,
    100, 102, 122
imagery, 14, 122
imaginal symbol, 1–3, 58, 59, 68
imagination, 113, 122
imitatio Christi, 39
immortality, 20, 28, 56
incorruptibility, 73
Inferno, 100, 158
initiate, 20, 26, 32, 38–39, 43, 46–48,
    82, 83, 121, 123, 155–56
initiation, 11, 63, 100, 102, 119
intercession, 106, 121
intuition, 5, 113, 122

Jacob's Ladder, 26, 30, 32, 46
Jordan River, 47

Kenosis, 145
kivas, 17, 26, 55
Kogi, 55–56
kundalini, 38, 81

Lance of Light, The (exercise), 34
Litany of Light, The (exercise), 124
Living Flame, The (exercise) 50
logos, 73

Love, 49, 126, 153

magi, 68, 99
magical glyphs, 9–10
magical patterns, 10
magical symbols, 1–10
mandorla, 20, 69, 149
martyria, 18, 121
martyrs, 120, 121
Mass, 19, 41, 65, 103, 162
material symbols, 2
materialism, 115
mediators, 119
meditation, 3, 20, 22, 34, 40, 48, 50, 67,
    78, 90–95, 107, 110
metals, 26, 99, 106, 110, 111
Mount Moriah, 57
Mount of Ascension, 98
Mount of Crucifixion, 98
Mount of Olives, 61, 160
Mount of Transfiguration, 98
Mount Purgatory, 56, 100
Mount Sinai, 57
Mount Zion, 57
mysticism, 14, 43
mythology, 10, 37, 42, 130
myths, 1, 20, 47, 147

nave, 18, 66
nimbus, 45
nodes, 33, 57–60, 63, 98–99, 123
north, 60, 65, 71, 73, 76

ogdoad, 84, 87, 105
opposites, 20, 81, 87, 127
ordeal, 102–3
orders, 1, 50, 82, 107, 120–21, 160
orientation, 26–27, 106–17
otherworld, 102
Our Lady of the Crystals (exercise), 110
Our Lady of the Stars (exercise), 107

pagans, 123
Paradise, 41, 106, 154
Paradise of the Fathers, The (Isho), 41
Paradiso, 84, 100
paradox, 6, 7, 127
paten, 64, 95, 157

INDEX

path, 6, 38, 103, 104
Pawnee Indians, 16
Pentecost, 40, 86, 154
perfection, 13, 20, 21, 122, 151, 161
Peter, 63, 66, 85, 90, 105, 135, 159, 161
phoenix, 68
pillar, 15, 18, 25, 30, 35, 41–43, 72, 131–32, 141, 151
Pisces, 90
planetary being, 81
planets, 87, 99, 105, 106, 108, 109, 140
plants, 45
polarity, 19, 76, 80, 99, 127
polarization, 21
polyvalence of symbols, 8
prayer, 40, 41, 48, 69, 120
pregnancy, 16
profane, 119, 137
projection, 118
promised land, 43
prophecy, 116, 141, 143
protection, 42, 94, 103, 105, 117, 140, 142, 161
Protector, 120
prototypes, 47
psychology, 21, 119
Pueblo Indians, 26, 55
purgatory, 100, 102
purification, 8, 40, 48, 121

Qabalah, 9, 27–28, 105, 122, 134, 139
quicksilver, 106, 111

reattunement, 83, 84
rebirth, 16–19, 32, 63, 77, 84, 87, 135
recreation, 84, 149
redemption, 1, 10, 18, 28, 31, 32, 60, 65, 83, 123, 124, 151
regeneration, 21, 28, 31, 32, 65, 77, 103, 130, 135, 136, 150, 151
relatedness, 40
relics, 121
reliquary, 17, 103
repentance, 102
resonance, 9, 103, 120, 131
restoration, 5, 10, 33, 124, 147
resurrection, 19, 20, 28, 48, 77, 83, 85, 123

revelation, 33, 105, 156
rhythms, 4, 87, 91, 127, 131
Risen Christ, 44, 84, 85, 97
ritual, 9, 119, 124–27
rock, 17, 31
rod, 29
rose windows, 18

sacrament, 63
saints, 10, 44, 77, 82, 90, 99, 120–21
sanctuaries, 121
seasonal cycles, 18
Secret Gospels, The (exercise), 91
Sermon on the Mount, 127
serpent, 32, 46
serpent's head, 33
shamans, 27
shrines, 9, 131
six-pointed cross, 62, 69
Solomon's Temple, 37, 57, 131
solstices, 78
souls, 11, 42, 46, 58, 84, 98, 118, 160
Sphere of Creation, The (exercise), 22
spirits, 103, 118
spirituality, 103
spring, 56, 71, 77, 79, 84, 85, 149
staff, 25, 29, 30, 31, 64, 151
summer, 59, 71, 79, 86, 93
Sun Chalice, The (exercise), 67
sword, 15, 31, 32, 33, 37, 93
symbols, 1–10, 59, 68, 90, 108, 116, 120, 147

table, 64–65, 87, 136
temples, 9, 98
tombs, 17, 98, 102
Transcension, 86

UnderRealm, 14, 18–19, 84, 97–107, 117, 138, 140, 150
unknowability of God, 43

Venus, 61, 106, 109
vesica piscis, 20, 110, 149
via affirmativa, 43
via negativa, 43, 122

zodiac, 9, 76, 84, 87, 90

QUEST BOOKS

encourages open-minded inquiry into
world religions, philosophy, science, and the arts
in order to understand the wisdom of the ages,
respect the unity of all life, and help people explore
individual spiritual self-transformation.

Its publications are generously supported by
The Kern Foundation,
a trust committed to Theosophical education.

Quest Books is the imprint of
the Theosophical Publishing House,
a division of the Theosophical Society in America.
For information about programs, literature,
on-line study, membership benefits, and international centers,
see www.theosophical.org
or call 800-669-1571 or (outside the U.S.) 630-668-1571.

Related Quest Titles

The Cross and the Grail, by Robert Ellwood

Esoteric Christianity, by Annie Besant

The Genesis Meditations, by Neil Douglas-Klotz

The Hidden Gospel, Neil Douglas-Klotz

Jesus Christ, Sun of God, by David Fideler

A Rebirth for Christianity, by Alvin Boyd Kuhn

To order books or a complete Quest catalog,
call 800-669-9425 or (outside the U.S.) 630-665-0130.